Pantanal Wildlife

A VISITOR'S GUIDE TO BRAZIL'S GREAT WETLAND

James Lowen

www.bradtguides.com

Bradt Travel Guides Ltd, UK
The Globe Pequot Press Inc, USA

edition

I

First published March 2010
Bradt Travel Guides Ltd
23 High Street, Chalfont St Peter, Bucks SL9 9QE, England
www.bradtguides.com
Published in the USA by The Globe Pequot Press Inc,
246 Goose Lane, PO Box 480, Guilford, Connecticut 06437-0480

British Library Cataloguing in Publication Data
A catalogue record for this book is available from the British Library

ISBN-13: 978 1 84162 305 4

Photographs
Photographs by James Lowen (JL) – www.pbase.com/james_lowen –
with the exception of the following:
Juan Mazar Barnett (JMB); Fabiano Ficagna de Oliveira (FFdO); Kathy Gemmell (KG);
Arthur Grosset (AG); Emily Horton (EH); Charlene de Jori (CdJ); Ben Lascelles (BL);
Alex Lees (AL); Lucas Leizinger (LL); Andrew Moon (AM); Otto Plantema (OP);
Heinz Plenge (HP); William Price (WP); OS Octavio Campos Salles (OS); Rafael Teixeira (RT);
Joseph Tobias (JT); Edo van Uchelen (EvU); Luis Vicente Campos (LVC); Mike Unwin (MU);
Emilio White (EW); Andre Seale/Still Pictures (AS).

The following photographers supplied courtesy of Frank Lane Picture Library:
Theo Allofs/Minden Pictures (TA/FLPA); Luciano Candisani/Minden Pictures (LC/FLPA);
Frank W Lane (FWL/FLPA); Frans Lanting (FL/FLPA); Claus Meyer (CM/FLPA);
Pete Oxford (PO/FLPA); Fritz Polking (FP/FLPA); Ingo Schulz /FLPA;
Jurgen Christine Sohns (JCS/FLPA); Terry Whittaker (TW/FLPA); Martin Withers (MW/FLPA).

Front cover jaguar (FL/FLPA)
Back cover hyacinth macaws (JL)
Title page (from top to bottom)
campo flicker (JL); giant otter (JL); yacaré caiman (RT)

Maps
Malcolm Barnes
Source material kindly supplied by ITMB, Conservation International and Guyra Paraguay

Designed and formatted by Chris Lane, Artinfusion (www.artinfusion.co.uk)
Printed and bound in India

CONTENTS

ABOUT THE AUTHOR

James Lowen returned to his true love – South American wildlife – during a break from his career as an environmental policymaker for the British government. He wrote this book while based in Argentina, working as a wildlife writer, editor and photographer. James has contributed to a dozen books and writes regularly for magazines. He also edits *Neotropical Birding*, the only magazine that focuses exclusively on birdwatching in Latin America, and his photographs have been published in books, magazines, newspapers, brochures and websites worldwide. James was formerly a tropical conservation researcher, studying wildlife all over the world and racking up a long series of scientific publications. Today, in his spare time, he is an ecotourism consultant and a naturalist aboard an expedition cruise ship.

AUTHOR'S ACKNOWLEDGEMENTS

Many people, in many ways, helped me prepare this book. I thank them all for their assistance, without which the product would have been inferior. I am grateful to a herd of wildlife enthusiasts who provided advice on specific sites: Roger Barnes, Giuliano Bernardon, Rasmus Boegh, Luiz Vicente Campos, Hugo Castillo, Antonio Castro, Rob Clay, Carol Coelho, Judy Davis, David Fisher, Benedito Freitas, Jan Frumau, John Hall, Bennett Hennessey, Charlene de Jori, Alistair Kerlin, Colin Kilpatrick, Guy Kirwan, Lucas Leizinger, Andres Linale, Juan Mazar Barnett, Joaquim de Mello, Sandro Menezes, Jeremy Minns, Otto Plantelma, Josephine Pryor, Julián Quillén Vidoz, the late Cheryl Schorp, Paul Smith, Juliane Souza, Rafael Teixeira, Pieter Westra and Alberto Yanosky. In the Pantanal, Bianca Bernardon and Rafael Teixeira widened my eyes to the wealth of wildlife, and numerous lodge owners and managers facilitated the days and nights.

A flock of biologists were my 'go to' women and men for a raft of detailed queries on particular wildlife groups: Gilberto Avalos, Luiz Vicente Campos, Lucas Leizinger, Steven Lenaerts, Célio Magalhaes, Fabiano Oliveira, Domingos Rodrigues, Paul Smith, Hojun Song, Christine Strüssmann, Guy Tansley, Mogens Trolle and Johan van't Bosch. A quintet of committed conservationists – Thomas Brooks, Katrina Brandon, Kelle Koenig, Edward Lohnes and Russ Mittermeier – provided material on Conservation International's work in the Pantanal and helped with a source map. Oscar Rodas and Hugo Cabral helped with another source map. A paparazzi of photographer friends responded to my invitation to contribute images. I thank them all – and those whose work is used are specifically acknowledged at the front of this book.

Danny Edmunds introduced me to Bradt, where Hilary Bradt, Anna Moores and Adrian Phillips provided guidance. Mike Unwin was a sterling editor, and a joy to work with. But, above all, I thank my travelling companion, note-taker, interpreter, videographer and wife, Sharon Lowen. Without her, this book would simply never have happened.

BRAZIL
BOLIVIA   The
Pantanal
PARAGUAY

SOUTH
AMERICA

0   160km
0   100 miles

Cuiabá

Cáceres

Poconé

Rondonópolis

MATO GROSSO

Porto Jofre

BOLIVIA

PANTANAL

B R A Z I L

Puerto Suárez

MATO GROSSO DO SUL

Quijarro   Corumbá

N

Bradt

Bahía Negra

Miranda

Aquidauana

Campo
Grande

PARAGUAY

KEY to maps on pages 120, 138 and 144

Pantanal

National boundary   — · —

State boundary   – – –

Road

Airport (international)   ✈

Urban Area

Town   ●

Village   ○

Lodge   ■

KEY for this map

Approximate area
of the Pantanal

Major road

Major urban area   ●

National boundary   — · —

State boundary   – – –

INTRODUCTION

The Pantanal is to the Americas what the Serengeti is to Africa. The aquatic heart of South America showcases some of the most breathtaking gatherings of mammals, birds and reptiles that you could ever hope to see. The numbers in the world's largest wetland can challenge credulity, with the smallest of lakes often so crowded with fur, feather and scale that you'll be pushed to spot an uninhabited metre of water. The Pantanal, in short, is a wildlife-watcher's paradise.

And it's not just any old bird or mammal that joins the throng. This immense wetland oozes quality as well as quantity. Record breakers of the natural world stalk, swim, slither, soar and skulk across the region. Every visitor wants to spot the largest cat in the New World (the jaguar), which is more easily seen in the Pantanal than anywhere else. And while this cannot be guaranteed, every visitor definitely *will* see the world's largest rodent (the pig-sized capybara). Also on display are the world's largest parrot (the electric-blue hyacinth macaw), the world's biggest snake (green anaconda), the continent's heaviest land mammal (South American tapir) and the world's largest gathering of crocodiles (yacaré caiman).

A typical Pantanal sunset over palm savanna alongside a watercourse. (HP)

This swarm of superlatives is matched by diversity. Some 475 species of bird and 135 mammals have been recorded on the Pantanal plains, along with 80 reptiles, 50 amphibians and perhaps 325 fish. And the voyages of biological discovery are far from over. In a recent survey of Pantanal fish, one-quarter of the 200 species found were new to science. Similarly, botanists surmise that the 1,700 plant species so far identified represent a mere half of the actual total.

Whatever your particular wildlife interest, there is masses to see. Much is out in the open – almost within touching distance and easily within reach of a camera. And the longer you stay, the deeper you can delve. If you like birds, seek out the chestnut-bellied guan – a pheasant-like creature on the road to extinction that occurs almost exclusively within the northern Pantanal. If smaller flying creatures are your thing, look for a butterfly with the eyes of an owl, the Illioneus giant owl, or drop to your knees and get a buzz from the emergence of thousands of winged termites at the tip of your nose. If mammals tickle your fancy, look to the trees for five species of monkey or wander the scrubby grasslands for four types of deer. And if it's life in cold blood that floats your boat, try to keep up with fleet-footed spiny lizards then catch your breath by enjoying the orchestrations of the nightly frog chorus.

This fantastic diversity derives from the region's position as a biogeographical melting pot. The Pantanal imbibes influences as diverse as Amazonia, Atlantic forest, Chaco and Cerrado. It then masticates them with highly seasonal rainfall to create a perpetually dynamic environment. Water – its presence or absence, its ebb or flow – is fundamental to all Pantanal life. After the summer rains, rivers burst their banks, spreading nutrient-bearing liquid over parched grasslands. A giant sponge, the Pantanal holds water for months, gradually releasing it towards the Atlantic Ocean. If the Amazon forests provide South America's lungs, then the Pantanal is the continent's kidneys. As waters subside and winter materialises, so a once abundant commodity becomes a prized resource. Fish become trapped in ever-shrinking lakes, attracting an abundance of herons and egrets. Capybaras keep cool by immersing themselves. Caimans – South America's crocodiles – jostle for space in the shallows to avoid dehydration. The dry season is show time and we visitors are the privileged audience.

A mere 50 years ago, Pantanal wildlife was cherished in a different way: as a resource to be exploited. Poachers killed countless otters and ocelots to provide fur for fashion. Egrets and caiman suffered the same fate for their feathers and skins. Trappers plundered populations of hyacinth macaws and other parrots to supply the cage-bird trade with its living trophies, forlornly incarcerated. There was money in wildlife – as long as it could be removed from the Pantanal.

Against this background, it is remarkable that wildlife-based tourism ever took off. But taken off it has. Unknown in the Pantanal until the 1980s, wildlife-watching is now big business. New lodges open every year, wildlife-viewing facilities constantly improve and access becomes easier. Ever more landowners recognise that wildlife is an asset to maintain not exploit. We have finally learnt to place value on the wild and living animal, rather than the captive or dead one. Our reward for this realisation? The finest wildlife experience in South America.

Yacaré caimans abound in the Pantanal's wetlands. (JL)

ABOUT THIS BOOK

This book aims to be a 'one-stop shop' for wildlife-watchers visiting the Pantanal. It is designed to address visitors' principal needs: to understand where they should go and what they are seeing. This guide has no pretensions to be a specialised field guide that enables you to identify every animal you encounter. Instead, it looks across the wildlife spectrum, aiming to sate your curiosity about a critter you have just seen – or want to see – without forcing you to fill your luggage with a shelf-full of weighty tomes.

The bulk of the book comprises four chapters that cover the most visible wildlife groups: *Mammals* (pages 19–50); *Birds* (pages 51–88); *Reptiles, amphibians and fish* (pages 89–104); and *Invertebrates* (pages 105–18). Engaging vignettes encompass ecology, behaviour and conservation as well as identification, bringing to life the Pantanal's characteristic and charismatic creatures.

The enormous, lofty nest of a pair of jabirus is a quintessential Pantanal sight. (JL)

Shorter chapters contextualise the wildlife experience. The *Pantanal environment* (pages 7–18) sets out the lie of the land, explaining what makes the Pantanal a wildlife haven and discussing its key habitats. *Top tips* (pages 151–62) offers suggestions as to how to find Pantanal wildlife, when to travel and what to bring. A *Further information* section (pages 163–6) identifies some specialised resources to help you plan and enjoy your trip.

A true traveller's companion needs to go beyond the 'what', and to encompass the 'where' and 'how'. Treating the Pantanal in its three-country entirety, *Where to go* (pages 119–50) details the best areas in which to search for the region's wildlife specialities. With helpful synopses of top lodges and advice on how to get around, this section provides everything you need to arrange your trip. In sum, this guide intends to make Pantanal animals real and to make your wildlife-watching life easier.

WHAT'S IN A NAME?

Ascribing names is a fundamental trait of human behaviour, reflecting our need to communicate and also, perhaps, our desire to order (and thereby 'own') confusing external entities. Biologists are no different from the rest of us, and have developed a honed system for naming organisms and defining their place in the natural world. This is called taxonomy or classification, and a grasp of its basic principles will help you understand the flow of this book.

The highest tier in nature's hierarchy is called a kingdom. Kingdoms are very broadly delineated, for example into animals, plants or fungi. The subsequent two layers – phyla (phylum in the singular) and subphyla – remain high-order divisions. All creatures with a

The rufous-tailed jacamar is a confiding bird of Pantanal forests. (JL)

backbone (commonly known as vertebrates), for instance, are housed in the animal kingdom, phylum Chordata and subphylum Vertebrata.

Within the vertebrates, conventional taxonomy recognises five classes, and these constitute the bulk of this book: mammals, birds, reptiles, amphibians and fish. Each subsequent taxonomic division is progressively more tightly defined, through orders, families and genera (singular: genus) until the organism is identified as a species. For complex groups, taxonomists sometimes use intermediate ranks such as suborders, subfamilies and subgenera. To take a Pantanal example, the black-tailed marmoset belongs to the class Mammalia, order Primates, suborder Haplorrhini ('dry-nosed' primates), family Cebidae (one of four families of New World monkeys), subfamily Callitrichinae (marmosets and tamarins), genus *Callithrix* (one of several marmoset genera) and subgenus *Mico*.

This hierarchy can seem confusing. To make things easier, each species has a scientific name, which consists of just two elements: the genus and species, which is written in italics, with the genus capitalised. The black-tailed marmoset referred to in the previous paragraph is thus known as *Callithrix melanura*. The advantage of scientific names is that they constitute a universal language that transcends international borders – unlike common names, which vary between and sometimes within countries.

A dawn mist dissipates to reveal tourist fishing boats on a Pantanal river. (HP)

The scientific name often derives from some aspect of the animal's appearance or habitat, from its geographical range or even from its human discoverer. In the Pantanal, for example, a common sight in forest is the rufous-tailed jacamar *Galbula ruficauda*, a bird whose specific name divides into *rufi* (meaning rufous) and *cauda* (meaning tail). Walking the trails, we may start at a Mato Grosso lancehead *Bothrops mattogrossensis*, a snake with a range centred on the eponymous Brazilian state. At night, we may chance upon an Azara's night monkey *Aotus azarae*, named after Félix de Azara, a Spanish military officer who catalogued central South American wildlife during the 18th century.

THE PANTANAL
ENVIRONMENT

The glorious blooms of the piúva tree bring colour
to Pantanal forests from July to September. (MU)

GEOGRAPHY AND GEOLOGY

The Pantanal is the world's largest contiguous wetland. Estimates of its size vary, but most fall in the range of 140,000–210,000km² – somewhere between that of Greece and Guyana. Around three-quarters of the Pantanal lies in west-central Brazil, divided between the states of Mato Grosso (40%) and Mato Grosso do Sul (60%). Of the remainder, two-thirds is in Bolivia and a third in Paraguay.

This whole vast expanse lies in a sedimentary basin surrounded by uplands: the Serras do Bodoquena and Maracajú to the south; the Brazilian *planalto* (plateau) to the east; the Matogrossense equivalent to the north; and the Serra do Amolar and Maçico do Urucum to the west. It is tempting to think of the Pantanal – from *pântano*, Portuguese for swamp – as one big wetland, but the region is far from homogeneous, and comprises ten or so large rivers and their deltas, plus thousands of lakes, interspersed with different types of grassland and forest.

The principal river is the Paraguay; this joins the Paraná 2,500km to the south before both emerge into the La Plata and reach the Atlantic Ocean in Argentina. Other major rivers include the Taquari, Miranda, Negro, Cuiabá and Aquidauana. All are slow-flowing and, during the rainy season (see *Climate*, below), burst their banks to flood large areas of low-lying plains. Only higher areas – formed by ancient dunes and now often covered with forest – remain dry. Altitude varies only from 80–150m throughout the upper Paraguay basin. The barely perceptible gradient rarely exceeds a 20cm drop in altitude per kilometre, slopes falling westwards and southwards.

The River Negro in Mato Grosso do Sul, Brazil, named for its black waters. (LL)

Even during the dry season, the *salinas* characteristic of Mato Grosso do Sul, Brazil, provide valuable sources of water. (LL)

CLIMATE

The nature of a visitor's wildlife experience in the Pantanal depends hugely on the season. A dry season visit differs so greatly from a wet season visit – in landscape, species and numbers – that you might imagine you were in an entirely different place. The key is rainfall distribution and timing. As a whole, the Pantanal receives 1,000–1,600mm of rain per year, predominantly between November and March. There are differences across the region – the south tending to receive less precipitation and in less concentrated form – and from one year to the next.

During the rainy season, rivers overflow and – together with fish and other aquatic wildlife – disperse across the plain to inundate 25–75% of the Pantanal. The flooded area can be ten times larger than the world's most famous wetland, Florida's Everglades, and 15 times the size of the best-known wetland for watching wildlife, Botswana's Okavango Delta. Water levels rise by up to 5m, soil nutrient levels increase and aquatic vegetation blooms. Dry land is at a premium, and higher areas (in Brazil, called *caapões* if small or *cordilheiras* if sizeable) hold concentrations of terrestrial mammals. Humidity rises from a winter mean of 62% (June) to a sticky summer figure of 80% (February). As the months pass, temperatures rise to 40°C from their mean of 25°C. Gradually, the tables turn. As temperatures reduce – falling to 7°C during winter cold snaps, when Antarctic air races north – terrestrial animals spread out and water becomes the precious commodity. Fish and other aquatic creatures are trapped in a dwindling number of shrinking water bodies, which become magnets for piscivores such as caimans and herons.

The pulse of the flood affects the Pantanal at different times. As rivers move from north to south, water levels peak four months earlier in the north than the south. By the time the south is fully flooded, the north has started its dry season. In the north, water levels respond quickly to rainfall, but flood retention smooths the peaks and troughs in the south. Flood intensity is also subject to multi-year cycles, with periods of extensive flooding alternating with more meagre periods.

When floodwaters recede, they often leave a 'tidemark' on trees. (JL)

THE HUMAN CONNECTION

People have inhabited the Pantanal for 5,500 years, but we know most about indigenous residents of the last millennium. Some lived on the Cerrado plateau but made hunting forays to the plains. Others, such as the Payaguá, Mbayá-Guaicurú and Guató, resided on islands within what was then an enormous lake, the Sea of Xaraes, subsisting by fishing. During the 16th and 17th centuries, Spanish and Portuguese colonialists traversed the region in their quest for El Dorado and initiated a long decline in native cultures. Today, few Guató remain, although the Mbayá-Guaicurú (represented by their descendants, the Kadiwéu) retain title to a reserve granted by the Portuguese in gratitude for their help in ousting the Spanish.

The discovery of alluvial gold accelerated colonisation. Towns such as Corumbá, Cuiabá and Cáceres sprang up to meet the need for secure trading bases. To furnish their taste for meat, the colonialists imported cattle during the 18th century. The bovines thrived and, by the early 20th century, beef exports – corned and dried – boomed. The same period marked the heyday of the trade in wildlife commodities: peccary skin for gloves, otter fur for coats and egret feathers for hats. *Pantaneiros* (Pantanal folk) were making a considerable living by plundering the land.

But all good things come to an end. While descendants of the ranchers plumped for the bright lights of coastal cities, their parents' cattle suffered a double whammy of drought and disease. By the 1980s, the frangible equilibrium between nature and

nourishment developed by the *pantaneiros* was out of kilter. Outsiders moved in, bringing disharmonious land management techniques. They cleared forest to create additional pasture – 500,000ha in the final quarter of the 20th century – and cultivated exotic grasses laced with herbicides. Not content with the well-established Nelore cattle (*Bos indicus*), incomers introduced water buffalo (*Bubalus bubalis*) as an alternative.

Despite subsequent economic diversification (to include mining, horticulture and tourism), cattle-ranching remains the bedrock of the *pantaneiro* lifestyle, with 80% of land devoted to the activity. Cattle roam widely, accompanied by the traditional *peões* or *peóns* (cowboys), whose way of life fascinates many visitors and forms an integral part of any Pantanal trip.

No *pantaneiro* is ever without a machete. (JL)

Estimates of the Pantanal's human population vary as widely as approximations of its area. A rough total for the Brazilian sector was 1.6 million in 1991, forecast to rise to 3.4 million by 2025 – around the same as the current cattle herd. This burgeoning population will inevitably place ever-greater demands on the Pantanal's natural resources. In addition to habitat loss, the great wetland has to contend with increasing pollution by run-off from

In the dry season, cattle are driven up the Transpantaneira highway in search of water. (JL)

Dry season fires burn swathes of vegetation, leaving only termite mounds standing. (JL)

mining and agriculture. Uncontrolled fires are frequent. Two of the world's most destructive invasive alien species – the giant East African snail (*Achatina fulica*) and Chinese golden mussel (*Limnoperna fortunei*) – lurk in Pantanal wetlands. One major development project, the Manso hydro-electric dam, has already altered the natural hydrology of the Cuiabá River. The plans for *Hidrovia*, a Paraguay–Paraná waterway that would have connected Bolivia with Uruguay, were shelved in the late 1990s. But its spectre has not been entirely vanquished.

PANTANAL MYTHS

As people developed their relationship with the Pantanal over centuries of living there, many myths and legends emerged. The mermaid-like *mãe d'água* ('mother of the waters') combs her hair atop a river rock. She protects river fish, so luckless fishermen ascribe their barren days to having hooked her blessing rather than any fish. Pantanal

Fishing is a key subsistence activity. (OP)

rivers are also reputedly inhabited by the *minhocão* or *minhocuçu*, a giant earthworm-like monster. So protective is the *minhocão* of its tranquil environment that, when disturbed by noisy fishermen, it emerges from its watery lair, destroying riverside huts, capsizing fishermen's canoes and even changing river courses. As if this were not enough for poor fishermen, they are also susceptible to pranks played by *negrinhos d'água*, mysterious 'Indians of the waters', who trawl the waterways in groups, looking for fishers to drag down to the river bottom and tickle.

Landowners are keen to conserve hyacinth macaws, in part as a tourist attraction. (JL)

CONSERVATION

It is not only wildlife and the *pantaneiro* way of life that run the combined gauntlet of these anthropogenic pressures. The stakes are higher and the vested interests more wide-reaching. At its peak, the Pantanal comprises 3% of the world's freshwater wetland area. It purifies water, recharges groundwater supplies and provides the huge downstream population with massive economic benefits that have yet to be calculated. The wetland also abates floods and provides arteries for commercial transportation. And it soaks up carbon dioxide, doing its bit in the battle against climate change.

Given these valuable contributions, it is a relief to know that at least part of the Pantanal enjoys protected status. State and private protected areas cover one-fortieth of the Brazilian Pantanal, with several ranches in Mato Grosso do Sul deriving financial benefit through wildlife tourism for conserving their natural resources. In Paraguay, the 123,000ha Río Negro National Park complements 77,000ha of private reserves (which welcome ecotourists – see *Where to go*, pages 144–8). Finally, around 600,000ha of the Bolivian Pantanal is ostensibly safeguarded in parts of two large protected areas (Otuquis and San Matías) and a small reserve owned by a local NGO. International NGOs such as Conservation International are thinking bigger, working with local partners to draw up plans for an 800km biological corridor linking Pantanal and Cerrado. There are also species-specific conservation programmes, including two focusing on the Pantanal's key flagship animals: jaguar and hyacinth macaw.

HABITATS

Extending across four major South American biomes, the Pantanal displays a mosaic of distinct habitat types – including forests, seasonally flooded grasslands and permanent lakes – whose distribution follows topography and soil type. Forests tend to lie atop raised areas (*capões* or *cordilheiras*) with calcium- and magnesium-enriched soils. Grasslands and cerrado usually dominate low-lying areas with poor soils. A basic understanding of Pantanal habitats will help you decide where to look for specific animals. There is little point in looking for a capybara in deciduous forest, nor much chance of finding a woodpecker in a swamp. At a more subtle level, if you want to see a cock-tailed tyrant – a small, globally threatened flycatcher – you should scour tracts of shrubby cerrado in Mato Grosso do Sul rather than the Chaco-influenced scrub of Paraguay. Botanists identify 16 vegetation classes and at least 1,700 flowering plant species in the Pantanal; here we home in on the most important and easily recognisable.

WETLANDS

Water is as innate to the Pantanal's identity as to that of the sea. The seasonal rhythm of its presence and absence governs the distribution, reproduction and growth of all manner of flora and fauna, as well as the movements and behaviour of humans – residents and visitors alike. A mosaic of aquatic habitats, the Pantanal has several types of watercourse, each with its own vegetation and wildlife community.

Permanent rivers and streams form the basis of aquatic life. Sandbanks along wide rivers provide nest sites for terns and skimmers, and resting points for lolling capybaras

Water hyacinths congregate into floating islands called *camalotes*. (OP)

Giant waterlilies *(left, RT)* provide good habitat for the wattled jacana *(right; JL)*, aptly nicknamed lily-trotter.

and dozing jaguars. On the tributaries, otters and kingfishers make their home amidst free-floating plants, such as the lilac-flowered common water hyacinth or *aguapé* (*Eichhornia crassipes*), and carnivorous bladderworts (*Utricularia*) that float below the surface, feeding on small aquatic insects.

In permanent lakes – *baías* or *corixos* in Brazil – water hyacinth congregates into huge floating islands of vegetation (*camalotes*) that are home to wattled jacana and least bittern. Still waters in the western Pantanal harbour that Goliath of plants, the giant waterlily (*Victoria cruciana*). Its circular leaves, strong enough to support a capybara, may reach 2m in diameter, and its flower 30cm. The bloom lasts but two nights and changes colour from white to pink during its short life. The flowers of a smaller, closely related waterlily (*Nymphaea*) open only at night, exuding a pungent scent.

Marshes and swamps are seasonal, expanding or contracting with floods and droughts. They are typically fringed with burheads (*Echinodorus paniculatus*), aquatic ferns (*Certopteris pterioides*) and bulrushes (*Typha domingensis*), the stems (rhizomes) of the last creeping under the mud before growing upwards. In the muddy margins, the purple flower spikes of pickerel weeds (*Pontederia cordata*) provide colour until nibbled by ducks. Yacaré caiman and anacondas skulk in these vegetated shallows; a variety of herons and ibises stalk pointedly through the water; and marsh deer graze along the edge. As the dry season progresses, these waters become ever more precious and ever more densely populated, hosting the quintessential Pantanal spectacle of teeming mammals, birds and crocodilians jostling for space and food.

In Nhecolândia in Mato Grosso do Sul, brackish lakes or *salinas* exist alongside typical freshwater lakes. The salinity was formerly considered a residue from an arid period in the Pleistocene. However, it transpires that the same water table links saline and fresh lakes, suggesting that the saltiness results from a more recent concentration process. These lakes often heave with wildfowl and capybara, concentrations that frequently attract the attention of jaguars.

Savannas in the northern Pantanal are interspersed with forest islands. (JL)

SAVANNAS

Savannas encompass almost one-third of the Pantanal, the highest proportion of any habitat type. Most are open grasslands dominated by native grasses (*Andropogon*, *Paspalum* and *Setaria*) in the family Poaceae; these lack shrubs or trees, hence their Brazilian name *campo limpo*, which literally means 'clean field'. In low-lying areas (*vazantes* in Brazil), grasslands are seasonally flooded and termed *campo alagado* (wet savanna); sedges (*Cyperus giganteus*) are common. Grassland with occasional shrubs and trees is called *campo sujo* (dirty field). Typical shrubs include fruit-bearing plants such as *Annona* and guava (*Psidium guineense*). Grasslands are the battlefield for an incessant struggle between herbs and woody plants. In wetter areas or seasons, herbs and grasses have the upper hand. In drier areas or periods, cerrado trees, such as the sandpaper tree (*Curatella americana*), and short palms (*Bactris*) encroach. In areas that are dry in winter yet flooded in summer, stands of *carandá* wax-palms (*Copernicia alba*) form the palm savannas that are such a characteristic Pantanal sight.

Although they may look relatively uninteresting, grasslands are excellent places for watching wildlife. Greater rhea and red-legged seriema stride around on long legs, while pampas deer graze the open fields. Giant anteater and various armadillos trawl the termite mounds on raised areas with *Elionurus muticus* grass, passing groups of long-tailed ground-doves and seedeaters scuttling across the open ground.

CERRADO

Some biogeographers consider the Pantanal to comprise a seasonally flooded extension of the Cerrado, the wooded savanna that formerly dominated the plateau of central Brazil. This habitat typically comprises slim, twisted trees that grow 5–10m above herbaceous vegetation and grasses, and prefers elevated areas on well-drained, sandy soils with few nutrients and high aluminium levels. Dominant cerrado trees include the pequi (*Caryocar brasiliense*) – the nuts and fruit of which are popular human foods – and hardwoods such as *Qualea grandiflora* and *Pouteria ramiflora*, used for timber and firewood. Most are adapted to withstand regular dry season fires. Denser, taller woodland is called *cerrado*, and often contains *algarrobo* or *jatobá* (*Hymenaea stigonocarpa*) and *capitão* (*Terminalia argentea*). *Pantaneiros* harvest *jatobá* sap on a waning moon, as its minerals and proteins are thought to stimulate kidneys and ovaries. Trunks of the congeneric *Hymenaea courbaril* serve as kayaks. Cerrado wildlife is similar to that in savannas, but also includes the maned wolf and scarce birds such as the white-banded tanager.

FORESTS

Cerrado is not the Pantanal's only wooded habitat. The variety of floristic influences results in a batch of closed-canopy formations.

Rivers and streams are usually lined with a thin strip of gallery forest, the canopy topping 20m and the flora demonstrating affinities with Amazonian or Atlantic forests. Common trees include a palm (*Bactris glaucescens*), the ice-cream bean (*Inga vera*), with its long seedpods, figs (*Ficus dendrocida*) and cambará (*Vochysia divergens*). The last disperses its seeds via floodwater and so the tree's distribution expands during high-water years. *Pantaneiros* weave *cambará* leaves into brooms and hats, and use it to fight infections and asthma. The *novateiro* (*Triplaris americana*), easily recognised by bunches of red, tubular flowers, is inhabited and protected by red ants (*Comatogaster* sp.). *Pantaneiros* with a twisted sense of humour initiate newcomers to Pantanal life by asking them to fell the *novateiro* for

Gallery forests along secluded, slow-flowing rivers are great for wildlife-watching. (OP)

firewood; ants rush out and sting the lumberjack who swiftly abandons his mission, screaming in pain. It is perhaps little wonder that Bolivians call this species the *palo de diablo* (devil's tree).

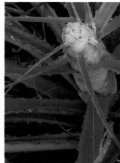

Forest forms: a strangler fig's twisted roots *(left)* and a spiky bromeliad *(right; both JL)*

Inside the forest, woody vines such as *Cissus spinosa* criss-cross above the sparse undergrowth. On damp ground nearby, *acuri* (*Scheelea phalerata*) and *bocaiúva* (*Acrocomia totai*) palm trees often dominate the understorey, their nuts a prized food for hyacinth macaws. Other prominent wildlife in gallery forests includes two monkeys – black howler and black-striped tufted capuchin – plus bare-faced curassow, and small birds such as helmeted manakin and cinereous-breasted spinetail.

Mesophitic (semi-deciduous and deciduous) forests grow on drier ground. In semi-deciduous forests, figs and *acuri* palms are also common, the latter often so tightly packed that they shade out shrubs. There are also *manduvi* (*Stercula apetala*) – the nest-tree for 95% of hyacinth macaws – silk trees (*Albizia niopioides*), gonçalo alves (*Astronium fraxinifolium*), aroeira peta (*Myracroduon urundeuva*) and persimmon (*Diospyros obovota*). Deciduous forests tend to be less dense, with large, spiky bromeliads (*Bromelia balansae*) often providing the only ground cover. In the southwest Pantanal, the Chacoan influence reveals itself with cacti such as the Peruvian apple cactus (*Cereus peruvianus*), which often reaches tree-like proportions, and prickly pear (*Opuntia stenartha*). In these forests, birdlife includes undulated tinamou on the ground, antbirds in the undergrowth, woodcreepers on the main branches and toucans in fruiting trees. Among mammals, look for lowland paca and Azara's agouti rooting in leaf litter, and Azara's night monkey and black-tailed marmoset among arboreal foliage.

Both mesophitic formations may be found as 'forest islands' – isolated woodlots slightly elevated above a seasonally inundated grassy plain that provide valuable refuges for ground-dwelling wildlife during floods. From July to September the most obvious trees are *lapacho* or *ypê* (*Tabebuia* sp.). The glorious blooms of these imposing trees may be yellow, pink or purple – depending on the species – and are the Pantanal's best-known floral spectacle. All flowers open simultaneously, a strategy that prevents birds such as the orange-backed troupial from eating the lot before they have served their pollination purpose. The pink ypê or *piúva* is Paraguay's national tree; its bark has medicinal properties that have prompted its commercialisation as *pau d'arco* tea.

MAMMALS

Southern tamandua. (JL)

Giant anteaters are a delightfully frequent Pantanal sight. (LL)

South America, like Africa, has a mammal 'big five' that wildlife-watchers dream of seeing: jaguar, maned wolf, giant anteater, giant otter and South American tapir. With effort, a judicious itinerary and a dose of luck, the Pantanal offers a good chance of clapping eyes on the entire quintet. There is no better place to see four of them, and there are a couple of good sites for the fifth (maned wolf). But even without these five biggies, the Pantanal provides the continent's best mammal-watching, with most visitors enjoying close views of a wide variety of species. In total, around 130 species occur.

ANTEATERS AND ARMADILLOS

Among the most bizarre mammals on the planet are undoubtedly members of the order Xenarthra. In a Pantanal context, these comprise two species of anteater (family Myrmecophagidae) and six armadillos (Dasypodidae). Their evolutionary connection is based on shared features such as modified vertebrae, a small brain and few, if any, teeth. The first of these characteristics provides the basis for their scientific name, Xenarthra being derived from the Latin for 'strange joints'. The third explains their former name of edentate, which derived from the Latin for 'toothless'.

ANTEATERS

With a long snout, small eyes, strong front claws and an extendable, sticky tongue instead of teeth, anteaters are supremely adapted for eating ants and termites. But such useful adaptations have their cost. To protect the front claws, anteaters must walk on their wrists. To survive on their low nutrition diet, they need a low metabolic rate and must sleep extensively – the record non-stop snooze lasting three days. And as the small mouth and hooked claws are no use for carrying offspring, a youngster must travel aboard its mother's back until it is old enough to fend for itself. Seeing an anteater is an undoubted trip highlight. The good news is that both species are relatively common in the Pantanal and active by day, so your chances of an encounter are good.

Giant anteater

Lumbering through grasslands on its daily trip to harvest termite mounds in its home range, a giant anteater (*Myrmecophaga tridactyla*) evokes awe and amusement in equal measure. Measuring up to 250cm from snout to tail and weighing more than 30kg, this is a big animal. But with its Pinocchio-like snout and shaggy tail, the 'ant bear' (as it is known in Spanish) has an undeniably comical demeanour.

A key use of the remarkable tail – which inspires the *pantaneiro* name of *tamandua-bandeira* (flag-anteater) – is to provide cover when the anteater is sleeping. On hot days, it provides shade; when cold, it conserves body heat. Anteater activity peaks in early evening, though they are out and about earlier on cold days – particularly in the forest patches, where temperatures are milder. With poor eyesight and hearing, a giant anteater depends on smell to locate ant and termite colonies. Using powerful forelimbs and hooked claws, it hacks into the hardened mound then – once it has made

The giant anteater uses its elongated snout to sniff out ants and termites. (TA/FLPA)

inroads – inserts its snout and extends a 60cm-long tongue coated with tiny spines and smeared with saliva. The tongue traps the colony occupants and, with a quick flickering motion, slurps them up the long vacuum cleaner-like snout. The meal ends with the arrival of the soldier ants or termites, which bite the intruder or release chemical secretions that force it to retreat – until the next day. By keeping its meals small rather than destroying the colony outright, the anteater maintains a sustainable resource.

Southern tamandua

In the Pantanal, an anteater up a tree is always a southern tamandua (*Tamandua tetradactyla*). An excellent climber, the tamandua uses its prehensile tail to improve balance as it reaches for arboreal termite mounds or bee nests, its fondness for the latter explaining the Spanish name *oso melero* (honey bear). The tamandua rips apart colonies or branches with its four sharp foreclaws, then inserts its elongated snout and long, sticky tongue to extract the tiny prey. If you hear ripping wood, you have probably chanced upon a tamandua. These animals are equally at home on the ground, however, where their two-tone pelage can be remarkably difficult to spot in the dappled light of an open woodland. Should a tamandua feel threatened, it may stand on its hind legs and sway its forelimbs from side to side, drawing attention to its sharp claws. The overall impression is of a punch-drunk boxer, but a single slash can inflict serious damage.

Of the two Pantanal anteaters, only the southern tamandua can climb trees. (JL)

ARMADILLOS

Few mammals appear more off-putting to a predator than armadillos. With bony armour-plating covering head, back and sides, there is no entry point for any but the wiliest of carnivores. This body armour, however, is the last line of armadillo defence: when sensing danger they prefer either to flee (preferably into thorny vegetation that does them no harm but impedes predators), or burrow to safety using their muscular front legs. The overlapping 'bands' of plates are separated at the mid-body by soft skin, thus allowing the armadillo to move.

Southern three-banded armadillo. (BL)

The Pantanal is home to a handful of armadillo species, ranging in length from 0.3–1.4m and in weight from 1–26kg. Most are shy and nocturnal, in part a legacy of poaching pressure. Visitors are most likely to bump into a nine-banded armadillo (*Dasypus novemcinctus*), hearing snuffling in pathside vegetation before the animal bumbles onto the track and into your torchlight. Stay still and this myopic mammal may approach closely, even wandering over your toes. Such an encounter will reveal its long nose, tail and ears, and may enable you to count its movable bands – one way to distinguish it from other armadillos (though beware that it can also have eight or ten bands). This species is an excellent excavator and leaves telltale diggings around its territory. It uses its long claws to bore its own burrows then lines the hole with leaves for comfort and insulation; this last process makes for an amusing spectacle, as the armadillo clasps the foliage under its body with its front legs and hops back to the burrow on its hindquarters.

Always seen by day, the six-banded armadillo (*Euphractes sexcinctus*) is omnivorous and even scavenges carrion. Otherwise solitary, individuals will congregate to feast on a carcass and the maggots that seethe over it. It is a chunky species and second in size only to the

The myopic nine-banded armadillo often allows close approach. (HP)

giant armadillo (*Priodontes maximus*). This latter is a near-mythical Goliath that eludes all but the most blessed visitor, being very rare (it is considered globally threatened), strictly nocturnal and spending most of its life underground. The giant armadillo is the nearest living relative of the glyptodonts – massive armadillos with a mace-like tail that died out during the last Ice Age.

At the bottom of the size spectrum is the southern three-banded armadillo (*Tolypeutes matacus*) that only just squeezes three armoured bands onto its stunted body. Like other armadillos, it flees when cornered, zigzagging away like a demented clockwork toy. Should it fail to escape, however, the armadillo has a unique defence. The front and back sections of its armour hang like a cloak, enabling it to roll into an impregnable armoured ball that denies predators access to its soft underbelly, now safely hidden inside the shell.

PRIMATES

The Pantanal is not overladen with primates, but this makes seeing one of its five species rather special. Currently allocated to a single family (Cebidae), each of these species sits in a separate genus. Recent taxonomy has preferred to increase the number of species rather than consolidate them (see box on page 26, *Splits, lumps and shuffles*) – a tendency that enhances mammal-watchers' interest in Pantanal monkeys.

The black-tailed marmoset (*Callithrix melanura*) is one result of this liberal approach to taxonomy, with its range almost entirely restricted to the Pantanal. Bird-like twittering and high, sibilant whistles in the forest draw the visitor's attention to a family of these diminutive monkeys busying themselves in the

A glimpse of dangling tail betrays a black-tailed marmoset among the foliage. (MU)

middle storey. Diurnal, arboreal and omnivorous, they readily gouge tree bark to extract sap and gum. This species is the only Pantanal primate that gives birth to twins rather than the standard single offspring.

Another primate whose presence is usually betrayed by its voice is the black howler (*Alouatta caraya*). An adult male's dawn roar, however, could not be less like the marmoset's demure chirping; easily carrying 3km, it is among the most distinctive Pantanal sounds. This is the region's largest monkey, about the size of a large house cat, but when silent it can be surprisingly unobtrusive. Families of up to ten munch quietly on leaves high in the forest canopy. Males are much larger than females, and young males take four years to attain the black pelage of adulthood.

The black-striped tufted capuchin (*Cebus libidinosus*) gets its English name from an order of Catholic friars who wore robes that covered their heads – although you need

The male black howler's dawn roar carries up to 3km. (JL)

considerable imagination to see its dark, erect crown tuft as a hood (see page 26). These monkeys achieved fame in 2004, when animals in northeast Brazil were the first non-ape primate to be seen using tools (in this case, cracking nuts on a stone anvil). Such behaviour has not (yet) been observed in the Pantanal, where troops of up to 40 animals feed primarily on arboreal fruit and seeds, but also search through leaf litter for invertebrates. Unlike the larger howlers, capuchins move and feed noisily, crashing through trees, and clucking, whistling or whining as the mood takes them.

Considerably smaller, but proportionately longer-tailed, is the white-coated titi (*Callicebus pallescens*), another recently 'emerged' species in a genus with convoluted taxonomy. Titis live in small groups each comprising a pair and their offspring from various years. These arboreal herbivores forage in dense vegetation, particularly near rivers, and spend long periods inactive, digesting food and conserving energy.

A view of Azara's night monkey by day reveals the large eyes typical of nocturnal species. (JL)

Aotus night monkeys are the New World's sole nocturnal primates. With luck, you may come across Azara's night monkey (*A. azarae*) by day as it roosts quietly in the sub-canopy. This primate's big brown eyes are framed by white crescents. At night, the monkey is quick to turn its small, round head away from torchlight, so all that you may see is a long, black-tipped tail, hanging perpendicular to a branch. On moonlit nights, this species gives a triple hoot that explains its alternative English name of owl monkey.

Taxonomic changes mean that black-striped tufted capuchin is now a species in its own right. (JL)

SPLITS, LUMPS AND SHUFFLES

For simplicity's sake, we present species names in this book as if they were set in stone. But taxonomic reality is not quite so immutable. When it comes to setting the limits for a particular species, biologists follow different schools of thought. In a process as ongoing as evolution itself, researchers propose 'splits' or 'lumps' whenever they consider species limits to be incorrect. Sometimes, evidence emerges that suggests that what were previously thought distinct species are actually so closely related as to be the same species ('lumping'). In the Pantanal, for instance, night monkeys (*Aotus* sp.) in Mato Grosso and Paraguay were formerly considered different species: now they are lumped together as Azara's night monkey (*A. azarae*). Alternatively, populations are sometimes adjudged to be sufficiently different that each merits elevation to the rank of full species ('splitting'). Sticking with primates, black-striped tufted capuchin (*Cebus libidinosus*) used to be brigaded with brown capuchin (*C. apella*), while black-tailed marmoset (*Callithrix melanura*) has only recently been hived off from silvery marmoset (*C. argentata*). Biologists cannot even always agree at the level of genus – supposedly a less confusing grouping. Cats are a case in point: should biologists treat New World felids conservatively as a mere five genera, or 'shuffle' them into as many as 18? In this book, we aim to follow the most recent biological consensus wherever it exists. But the only constant in taxonomy is that it is in permanent flux.

CARNIVORES

Wherever one travels to watch wildlife, carnivores tend to top the wish list. The Pantanal is no different, with two of the most charismatic mammals in South America – the jaguar and giant otter – both being flesh-eaters. With a few exceptions, such as China's bamboo-munching giant panda (*Ailuropoda melanoleuca*), members of the order Carnivora survive primarily by catching, killing and consuming other vertebrates. Many hunt opportunistically, preying on whatever crosses their path. Three broad groups occur in the Pantanal: dogs, cats and a wider agglomeration encompassing weasels, skunks and raccoons.

Crab-eating foxes often visit lodges, looking for scraps. (AM)

DOGS

The Pantanal hosts only four species of dog (family Canidae) but these include the continent's smallest and largest. The crab-eating fox (*Cerdocyon thous*) is the region's most common canid. As the name suggests, it has a taste for crustaceans, with crabs monopolising its diet during the rainy season. But there would be obvious drawbacks in depending entirely on a food resource that effectively disappears during the dry season. Accordingly, foxes

The rarely seen bush dog is the only South American canid to live in packs. (TW/FLPA)

Seeing a maned wolf – a fox on stilts – is a red-letter day. (EW)

also consume small mammals, reptiles and amphibians. They will also eat fruit, seeds and other plant material, and readily scavenge for scraps discarded by lodge kitchens. Such 'feeding times' are one way to get a good look at a crab-eating fox, with its distinctive short muzzle, truncated tail and black stripe along the spine. Pairs often forage in rough association, a few minutes apart.

If you are lucky enough to spot a long-eared fox on stilts, you have struck gold. At almost 1m tall, the unmistakable maned wolf (*Chrysocyon brachyurus*) is South America's largest canid. Routinely omnivorous, its diet is as likely to include fruit as rodents; wolf's apple (*Solanum lycocarpum*) is a particular favourite. The best chance of seeing this globally threatened carnivore is during the dry season in isolated cerrados, particularly in Mato Grosso do Sul.

At the opposite end of the size spectrum are two even rarer canids that, realistically, only those fortunate enough to live in the Pantanal stand a chance of seeing. The bush dog (*Speothos venaticus*) is the only New World canid to live in packs, members keeping in contact with yelps as they hunt lowland paca in forest undergrowth. The hoary fox (*Lycalopex vetulus*) hunts by day for cerrado insects and the odd rodent. This species is a cause for concern among conservationists but without adequate information with which to classify its status they have placed it the holding pen of 'Data Deficient'.

CATS

Cats (Felidae) are consummate carnivores, eating nothing but flesh. Supreme predators, they grab prey with sharp, retractile claws, and dispatch it with a bite to the neck. The Pantanal hosts an outstanding selection of felids, with eight species recorded. Six have a spotted pelage, varying in size from the domestic cat-sized oncilla (*Leopardus tigrina*) to the jaguar (*Panthera onca*), king of South America's jungle. Two are unmarked, the heftier being puma (*Puma concolor*). All eight are rare, solitary and largely nocturnal. Seeing any cat is thus a considerable challenge, but Pantanal researchers and guides are getting to grips with the behaviour and movements of several species. Accordingly, the Pantanal offers far better prospects of seeing jaguar – undeniably the most sought-after mammal in the New World – than anywhere else.

Jaguar

The jaguar is the largest cat in the Americas and the third largest worldwide, topped only by the tiger (*Panthera tigris*) and lion (*Panthera leo*). Deep-chested, large-headed and stocky, a male jaguar can measure 2.5m in length, including tail, and 130kg in weight – resembling a bodybuilding leopard. The Pantanal subspecies is the largest and heaviest – twice the size of those in Central America. It is hardly surprising that every visitor to the Pantanal wants to see one (see box, *How to find a jaguar*, page 156).

Jaguars are primarily forest animals with a fondness for riverbanks. They swim well, readily traversing rivers to move between forest tracts. Large carnivores need large prey populations that, in turn, require a large area of habitat. Jaguars thus have substantial home ranges, although those of several individuals may overlap. Estimates of Pantanal jaguar density vary from three to seven individuals per 100km², with densities higher (or home ranges smaller) during the wet season. Every jaguar has a different pattern of head markings, which enables researchers to track specific individuals with relative ease.

Seeing a jaguar would be the highlight of any visitor's Pantanal trip. (PO/FLPA)

Checking riverbanks from a boat is the best way to find a resting jaguar. (JL)

Jaguars are opportunistic and voracious predators, with virtually no animal being too much to handle. A powerful bite through the back of the skull is sufficient to subdue a cow three times the cat's weight. Robust canines can pierce even the protective armour of caimans, turtles and armadillos. Capybaras form much of the diet, and jaguars wait in ambush at favoured sites. Using whatever cover is available, they stalk their target to within pouncing distance. If this involves chasing the capybara into water and nabbing it before it dives to safety, so be it.

Like all Neotropical cats, jaguars are solitary. Sightings of two animals together almost always relate to a mother and offspring (which travel with one another until the youngster is 15–18 months old), or to a female in oestrus with an attendant wandering male. Pair bonds are brief and intense: jaguars may mate 100 times per day during the female's one to two-week fertile period. During the mating season, both sexes roar to attract each other's attention, a series of deep grunts that carries for 400m.

Conservationists have no clear idea how many jaguars are left, but know that the species is declining and at potential future risk of extinction. Fortunately, the poaching heyday of the 1960s – when 15,000 spotty pelts were exported from Brazil each year – is long gone as a result of legislation banning international trade. Direct persecution remains a threat, however, with some ranchers killing cats where they are thought to predate livestock. Odd landowners even go as far as to make money from shooting jaguars, charging sport hunters US$20,000 for a pop at a feline trophy. But the greatest threat to jaguars, as with so much of tropical biodiversity, is deforestation.

Other spotted cats

Should you not be fortunate enough to enjoy a jaguar, do not despair. You have five additional opportunities for a spotted cat experience, at a range of sizes. The ocelot (*Felis pardalis*) is roughly the size of a cocker spaniel. Relative to a jaguar, it also has a smaller head, larger ears and a more sprightly gait, and the spots on its neck and flanks coalesce into distinctive stripes. Ocelots are mainly nocturnal; the last hour of daylight is a prime time to see one. Prey consists mostly of terrestrial rodents, although Pantanal animals eat fish and even black howlers.

The Pantanal is a great place to see ocelot, particularly just before dusk. (FL/FLPA)

The margay (*Leopardus wiedii*) is dainty and long-tailed, with large rosettes on its flanks. It is the only spotted cat that routinely climbs trees; flexible ankle joints enable it to descend vertical surfaces head first. Only the luckiest visitor will see a margay, but your chances of oncilla (*L. tigrinus*) are higher. Built like a slim house cat, this felid has larger eyes and ears but a shorter tail than the margay. Geoffroy's cat (*L.*

The slender Geoffroy's cat. (JCS/FLPA)

geoffroyi) is more slender still, with distinctive small spots on a grey or brown coat. As this cat favours dry woodland, your best chance of seeing it is in Bolivia or Paraguay. Of similar size, but stockier and with striped chest and legs, is the Pantanal cat (*L. braccatus*), formerly considered a subspecies of the colocolo (*L. colocolo*). As its English name suggests, the core of this cat's range is the Pantanal.

Eye to eye with a puma. (FL/FLPA)

The jaguarundi is the only New World cat that has a range of pelt colours. (PO/FLPA)

Plain cats

If spots are now dancing before your eyes, take a breather with the two monotone species of felid in the genus *Puma*. Both are lithe creatures, with slim bodies and long tails, the jaguarundi (*P. yagouaroundi*) being so long-bodied and short-legged as to recall a member of the weasel family (Mustelidae). Indeed, you might easily confuse it with one such animal – the tayra (see page 36) – given that both are adept climbers. The jaguarundi is unique among American felids in exhibiting a wide range of pelt colours, with chestnut, brown, grey and black all common. The much larger puma (*P. concolor*) also varies in colour, but only between tawny and rufous. In dimensions, it falls only slightly shy of the jaguar, but it is a rangier, more lithe animal with a noticeably lighter tread. This cat has one of the largest ranges of any land mammal, extending from the Arctic Circle south to Tierra del Fuego. It is scarce in the Pantanal – perhaps because it cannot compete with the stronger jaguar – but you are, however, more likely to see one in drier, open areas such as grasslands, where it hunts mainly by night for small and medium-sized mammals. Visitors from North America know the puma as the mountain lion, panther or cougar. Indeed, across its huge range, this species is known by some 40 English names, more than any other animal.

OTTERS, WEASELS, SKUNKS AND RACCOONS

The Pantanal's other carnivores are divided among three families. Slinky of body and sinuous in movement, the Mustelidae family comprises otters, weasels and their allies. Though species vary in size, all share a similar general form: a long body with short legs and a comparatively short tail, and a broad head with small ears and eyes. Most species can hear and smell well, but see only poorly, which can be a boon if you observe them quietly from downwind. In the Pantanal, the family comprises two otters (subfamily Lutrinae) and two true mustelids (subfamily Mustelinae). Similar in some ways, skunks were formerly brigaded with mustelids but are now assigned their own family (Mephitidae), while the two species of raccoons belong to a third family (Procyonidae).

Giant otter

While glimpsing a jaguar may be the Pantanal nirvana, the trip highlight for most visitors is an hour spent in the company of a confiding family of giant otters (*Pteronura brasiliensis*) as they cavort and snort just a few metres away. Giant otters tick all the boxes required to be part of that exclusive club, South America's 'big five': they are undeniably big – up to 1.8m long and 35kg; they are impressive predators, all sleek muscularity underwater as they effortlessly catch their fishy prey; and they offer that irresistible blend of the elusive and the showy – hard to find (so raising the blood pressure) but consummate performers (so worth the effort). Finally, giant otters have rarity value, habitat destruction and persecution having caused populations to plummet so far that the species is classified as globally threatened.

Web-footed, dense-furred and with a broad, flattened tail that is encapsulated in its genus name (*Pteronura* deriving from the Greek for 'wing tail'), the giant otter is largely aquatic. Known in Spanish as *lobo del río* ('river wolf'), this species is a fan of slow-moving rivers with gently sloping banks and overhanging vegetation. If you whistle or gargle, an inquisitive otter may approach to check out the strange sounds. This should give you a

Giant otter are expert fishers, this one munching on a catfish. (JL)

Highly social creatures, giant otters are usually seen in groups. (JL)

good view of its pattern of cream blotches on the throat – unique to each individual – and of the formidable canines that give fish no hope of escape. Giant otters have a particular taste for catfish (Siluriformes) and characins (Characidae), which they consume noisily. Recently, a few individuals along the Pixaim and Claro rivers in Mato Grosso have grown bold enough to indulge human visitors by taking fish offered by boat drivers.

Giant otters are sociable creatures, living in cohesive families of up to eight individuals. Active by day, groups retreat to communal dens at dusk. These 'holts' are easy to spot: a wide hollow on the riverbank with a large landing beach cleared of vegetation but covered with webbed footprints. They are also highly audible animals, being the most vocal otter and the one with the widest repertoire. Gruff barks alert pack members to danger, a growl serves as a warning and a soft coo soothes. Wider social interactions appear to be less harmonious: researchers are finding evidence of fractious conflicts between neighbours at territory boundaries. Such intraspecific aggression is rare among mustelids and is presumably the flip side of strong bonds within a group.

Nevertheless, rival otters are less a source of danger than are humans. In the 1960s, more than 1,000 otters were killed each year in Amazonian Brazil alone. This compares to a current population, throughout the otter's entire range, that may be as low as 1,000 animals. Fortunately, poaching for pelts has declined dramatically with the enforcement of new legislation. But current threats are more insidious. Loggers clear rainforest and farmers move in, removing riverside vegetation and degrading water quality. In turn, this reduces the viability of increasingly fragmented subpopulations. No surprise that pessimistic conservationists have predicted a further 50% decline in numbers during the 20 years from 2004.

Neotropical otter

Compared with its giant relative, the Neotropical otter (*Lontra longicaudis*) is a mystery. The World Conservation Union classifies it as 'Data Deficient', which effectively means that it could well be in danger of extinction – but we simply don't know. This shroud of uncertainty increases the allure of this ostensibly less dramatic mustelid. Neotropical otters are less brawny than giant otters. They are also more catholic in their habitat requirements, inhabiting pretty much any watercourse. Such wide tastes help them avoid conflict with their larger cousin, as does their ability to fish at night. During the dry season, these solitary mammals disperse to find foraging grounds. Lucky visitors may come across an otter humping its way across land between far-flung water bodies, its head and tail distinctly drooped.

The Neotropical otter is too poorly known for biologists to agree on its conservation status. (OS)

Typical mustelids

At night, most carnivores' eyes glow orange when reflecting torchlight. Those of the tayra (*Eira barbara*) are the exception, facilitating identification by gleaming blue-green. However, you are more likely to see this active, powerful mammal by day. Tayras forage alone or in family groups, bounding through forests for up to 8km per day. They ascend trees to feast on fruit, snatch arboreal arthropods and rob bird nests, but are wary animals, fleeing at the first perception of a threat and growling aggressively as they leap away.

The final Pantanal mustelid, the grison (*Galictis* sp.), is smaller and longer-necked than a tayra, with a distinctive black, white and grey coat. Primarily nocturnal, it is rarely seen – which perhaps explains why mammologists are not entirely sure whether the Pantanal species is lesser grison (*G. cuja*), greater grison (*G. vittata*) or both.

Skunk

Molina's hog-nosed skunk (*Conepatus chinga*) is the one member of its genus found in the Pantanal, where it is readily identified by its bold black-and-white markings. Like other skunks, this nocturnal animal has the dubious claim to fame of being known principally for its odour, used as a defensive weapon. When a skunk feels threatened, it squirts sulphuric liquid from anal scent glands; the spray can reach 5m and the scent can drift 1.5km downwind.

Raccoons

The Pantanal's two members of the raccoon family (Procyonidae) split the 24-

Night drives offer the best chance of spotting a crab-eating raccoon. (JL)

hour clock between them: the South American coati (*Nasua nasua*) is exclusively diurnal and the crab-eating raccoon (*Procyon cancrivorus*) entirely nocturnal. The coati has a comical appearance. Its long, narrow snout ends in an upturned nose that constantly sniffs the air for food or threat, while white crescents around the eye lend the animal a startled look. Females and youngsters form large groups that troop noisily through the forest, banded

Tayras are equally at home in trees and on the ground. (AG)

South American coatis are fairly common, sociable mammals. (OP)

tails raised perpendicular to the body, tips swishing above the undergrowth. Coatis are opportunistic omnivores, climbing trees to harvest fruits or snuffling through leaf litter to unearth invertebrates. Groups signal danger with an abrupt bark, a cue for the members to scatter up trees from where they make a communal assessment of the threat.

With its bandit-like mask, short grey fur and faintly ringed tail, there is no mistaking a crab-eating raccoon. Individuals or pairs typically forage along the damp fringes of a watercourse, hunting any creature associated with wet habitats: from fish and amphibians to insects and, of course, crabs. During the dry season, they also devour other foods such as fruits. As day breaks, raccoons scuttle back to their dens, snugly sited in hollow trees.

SMILE FOR THE CAMERA – AND CONSERVATION!

Camera traps are now a 'must-have' gizmo for wildlife biologists across the world. Researchers install motion or infrared sensors in a location that they expect a rarely seen animal to visit. Movement trips these sensors, prompting the camera to take an image. In this way, biologists can gather useful information on the presence of species that might otherwise elude them. Pantanal biologists such as Mogens Trolle have taken this tool one step further, using it to calculate population densities for rare mammals. Realising that ocelot markings were different on every individual, Trolle was able to estimate that there are about 2.8 ocelots in every 5km². On the basis of densities of roughly 1.5 maned wolves per 100km² (the first ever published for the species), Trolle considers that this scarce canid may be coping better than expected with habitat fragmentation. If replicated throughout suitable habitat, South American tapir densities of 0.6 animals per 1km² would confirm the Pantanal's importance for this globally threatened ungulate.

UNGULATES

Ungulates (literally 'hoofed animals') comprise herbivores that walk on the tips of their hoofed toes. There are 'even-toed' ungulates (order Artiodactyla) and 'odd-toed' ungulates (order Perissodactyla). In even-toed ungulates, weight falls evenly between the third and fourth toes, which form a cloven hoof; a pair of smaller toes usually remain clear of the ground. Native families comprise peccaries (Tayassuidae) and deer (Cervidae). Odd-toed ungulates, by contrast, have a prominent third, central digit that bears the most weight. The best-known odd-toed ungulates are horses (Equidae), but their only native New World representatives are tapirs (Tapiridae).

South American tapirs extract minerals from mud wallows. (JT)

TAPIR

Only four species of tapir occur in the world, of which three are in the Neotropics (the other being in Indochina). By far the heaviest land mammal in South America, reaching 250kg, the South American tapir (*Tapirus terrestris*) would merit its place in the continent's 'big five' even without its rarity and bizarre looks. Due to incessant hunting and habitat destruction, this species is globally threatened, and seeing one is a near-impossible task – except in the Pantanal, where it is a regular feature on night drives. As for looks, the pony-sized tapir is in a class of its own, with an elongated proboscis of an upper lip and humped forehead that leads into a short, erect mane. The long snout is a boon for getting at vegetation and fruit, but the mane's purpose is less clear. Whereas adults are coloured a monotone grey, youngsters are striped chestnut and white, a resplendent garb that breaks up the animal's outline in shady forest, concealing it from the gaze of large cats. This shy tapir rarely strays far from woodland, and is most frequent close to water. A common sign of its presence is a waterside pile of seed-filled droppings.

PECCARIES

Scared of walking in the forest in case a jaguar pounces on you? Surprisingly perhaps, a more likely source of danger is the white-lipped peccary (*Tayassu pecari*). Peccaries

(Tayassidae) are the New World's answer to Old World pigs (Suidae), although they used to inhabit Eurasia until leaving it for South America three million years ago. While related, peccaries differ from pigs in terms of morphology and ecology. Pigs, for example, have large litters of helpless young, whereas peccaries usually have twins that are active from birth.

Peccaries are sizeable mammals, standing 50cm tall and 1m long, and weighing up to 45kg. They are front-loaded, with large heads and thick necks but a tiny tail. The head is tipped with a flexible snout that sniffs along the ground for fruit and seeds to supplement the main diet of foliage. The three Pantanal species are largely diurnal. One reason for the fear invoked by white-lipped

White-lipped peccary. (HP)

peccaries is that they gang up in herds that regularly exceed 100 animals. Should a herd feel threatened, members make a fearsome racket by collectively clattering their canines. Should this not encourage the intruder to retreat, larger individuals may charge. Fortunately, peccaries see poorly, so they tend not to notice a silent, stationary human. Watching a hundred peccaries file past at close range is an exciting experience, but because white-lipped peccaries are semi-nomadic, seeing them requires either luck or up-to-date local knowledge.

The Pantanal's two other peccaries, collared peccary (*Pecari tajacu*) and Chacoan peccary (*Catagonus wagneri*), congregate only in single figures. Collared peccaries are wary, hiding in dense cover during the day, fleeing when sensing danger and leaving a strong cheese-like odour in their wake – the origin of their colloquial name of 'musk hog'. The shaggy-maned Chacoan peccary just sneaks into the Paraguayan Pantanal. This is one of very few living mammals described for science on the basis of fossils. Thought extinct until its 'rediscovery' by scientists in 1975, it transpired that native inhabitants had known about it all along.

Beware that not every swine you see in the Pantanal is a peccary: large numbers of feral pigs (*Sus scrofa*) also wander through forest and grassland. The head and jaw structure of these alien invaders enables them to root more efficiently, suggesting that, over time, they might outcompete the native peccaries.

White-lipped peccaries often travel in sizeable herds. (EW)

DEER

Originating in Eurasia, deer (Cervidae) reached South America during the late Pliocene (1.8–5 million years ago), whereupon different species evolved rapidly to fill different niches. Four species inhabit the Pantanal, two each in open areas and scrubby forests. All are large, graceful animals with long limbs. Males grow and shed antlers each year. Deer feed exclusively on vegetable matter: after eating, they must rest, regurgitate and ruminate – like cud-chewing cattle.

The largest is a giant. Standing 1.2m tall and 2m long, male marsh deer (*Blastocerus dichotomus*) have thick, branching antlers 60cm in length. These deer inhabit long grassland or dense reeds near standing water. They have hooves that spread to maximise the area of contact in slippery or soft terrain – an adaptation for life in wet habitats. Inevitably, marsh deer distribution in the Pantanal shifts with the season: animals disperse widely during floods, but concentrate near water during the dry period. The marsh deer has become very rare and localised as a result of habitat destruction, hunting and infection with cattle diseases. Nevertheless, this globally threatened cervid is fairly common in the Pantanal, and most visitors should see it.

Marsh deer – here a young female – are in danger of extinction. (JL)

The pampas deer (*Ozotocerus bezoarticus*) is best distinguished from the marsh deer by its smaller size, chestnut (rather than black) lower limbs, obvious white eye-ring and, in males, simpler antlers. The English names also convey the habitat preferences of the two species, pampas deer preferring dry grasslands, where they browse herbs. Populations have not yet recovered from massive hunting in the 19th century when, for example, more than 60,000 skins were exported from Buenos Aires in 1880. In consequence, conservationists consider this species at possible future risk of extinction.

The small size and short antlers of the Pantanal's two brocket deer (*Mazama* sp.) are probably adaptations for efficient movement through dense woody vegetation. Brocket deer are primarily shy and nocturnal, but may be diurnal and confiding where not hunted. Unlike the two larger deer, which often feed in small groups, the brockets live alone or in monogamous pairs. The South American red brocket (*M. americana*) differs from the South American brown brocket or grey brocket (*M. gouazoubira*) by coat colour and its preference for moister, denser forest.

South American brown brocket deer prefers dense, moist forest. (JL)

Common vampire bats are responsible for bats' ghoulish reputation. (JL)

BATS

In the Western world, bats have a ghoulish image, largely because of their reputation as bloodsuckers. The reality is rather different, with most bats playing a critical ecosystem role as pollinators, seed dispersers and consumers of insects. Nevertheless, behind every fear lies a smidgeon of justification, and so it is with New World bats, among which are the perpetrators of those bloodsucking phobias, the vampire bats (*Desmodus*).

Bats are so evolutionarily distinct as to be allocated to their own order, Chiroptera. Their ability to fly has enabled them to exploit a large variety of food resources and thus to evolve into a significant variety and number of forms. The majority of Neotropical species are insectivores, but others consume fruit, fish, pollen, frogs, birds, crustaceans and, of course, mammalian blood. Bats are exclusively nocturnal. Hunting in darkness requires special skills, and all Neotropical bats home in on their target by using echolocation. The bat uses its mouth or flaps of skin on its nose to amplify high-pitched clicks, and captures returning echoes with its large ears. From this information, it constructs an auditory 'picture' of its surroundings. Each bat family has its own echolocation system, with distinctive morphological structures that emit and gather aural data that only that family can interpret.

There are 35 Pantanal bat species in five families. Distinguishing them is difficult, but, fortunately, some are distinctive. A score of bats arranged in vertical lines on a sunlit riverside tree trunk, for example, will be proboscis bats (*Rhynchonycteris naso*). Named for its elongated nose, this species is one of two members of the Emballouridae family. Diagnostic white tufts on its forearms and an overall frosted coloration help it blend into the lichen-covered trunk, thereby offering camouflage against predators. Unsurprisingly for a species that tolerates daylight, the proboscis bat is active early in the evening, hunting aerial insects low over water bodies.

The frosted pelage of proboscis bats offers camouflage. (IS/FLPA)

BULLDOG BATS

Another bat family – the Noctilionidae – has an even closer relationship with water. As the skies darken, those above Pantanal rivers fill with two species of bulldog bat (*Noctilio*), which soon descend on pointed wings to skim the water surface. These relatively big bats have long legs and sharp-clawed feet, with which they snatch prey from the water. Of the two species, the lesser bulldog bat (*N. albiventris*) is smaller, emerges earlier and feeds on aquatic insects. The greater bulldog bat (*N. leporinus*) catches fish; hence its alternative English name of greater fishing bat. This species has such precise echolocation that it can pinpoint tiny fish from the slightest of ripples. It may catch 30 fish in a night, storing them in bulldog-like cheek pouches before returning to the colony.

LEAF-NOSED BATS

Leaf-nosed bats (Phyllostomidae) are named after the spear-shaped fold of skin that flares above their nostrils. Members of this diverse group differ so markedly in size, shape, feeding habits and sociality that the family is a microcosm for the order as a whole. The Pantanal hosts 13 species in almost as many genera. The most infamous is the common vampire bat (*Desmodus rotundus*), which is morphologically equipped for its specialised niche. Blade-shaped teeth make a painless incision in the skin of their sleeping prey, while an anticoagulant in the saliva enables the bat to lap up the free-flowing blood. The Pantanal's main economic activity has been a boon for this bat, which targets cattle as more convenient blood banks than wild ungulates. *Pantaneiros* accuse vampires of being vectors for rabies, and tend to kill them. Another bat with a taste for flesh is the greater round-eared bat (*Tonatia bidens*), which grabs small birds while they roost. One of the New World's largest bats, the greater spear-nosed bat (*Phyllostomus hastatus*) uses its bulk to capture small rodents and even other bats before returning to its tiny colony.

Seba's short-tailed bats are among several fruit-eating species that play an important role in seed dispersal. (JL)

Some members of this group differ markedly in social and foraging behaviour. Pallas's long-tongued bat (*Glossophaga soricina*) forms nurseries of several hundred females and their young. It routinely hovers by flowers, using its long muzzle and tongue to extract nectar and pollen, but also gleans insects from the underside of leaves. Sugar is a precious resource so bats defend nectar-producing *Agave* plants against rivals. Another valuable 'resource' is a mate – or several. Male Seba's short-tailed bats (*Carollia perspicillata*) guard harems of females. This is one of several frugivorous bats that disperse seeds, thus helping regenerate the forest. The Pantanal's largest frugivore is the great fruit-eating bat (*Artibeus lituratus*). By day, it roosts under 'tents', made from leaves nibbled into a protective shape.

INSECTIVOROUS BATS

Nectarivory and frugivory are actually rather rare in the bat world. The vast majority of bats eat insects. The family Vespertilionidae houses the Pantanal's trio of myotis (*Myotis* sp.), which fly rapidly and with agility around forest clearings, using their large tail membrane to scoop up tiny insects. The black myotis (*M. nigricans*) synchronises its breeding cycle with periods of insect abundance, with females able to store sperm until the time is right.

The Pantanal has a dozen species of free-tailed or mastiff bat (Molossidae). These fly swiftly and erratically on narrow wings high in the sky, foraging for large insects. The alternative English names relate to the bats' appearance: a dog-like face (hence mastiff) and a long tail extending beyond its membrane (free-tailed). But these are not the family's only peculiarities: the flattened bodies of species such as Pallas's mastiff bat (*Molossus molossus*) allow large numbers to roost packed together in confined spaces such as roofs.

RODENTS AND RABBITS

Rodents (order Rodentia) are a great mammalian paradox: they comprise nearly half the world's mammal species, yet most are very rarely seen. The reasons for this discrepancy lie in their basic ecology: rodents are generally shy, small, nocturnal creatures that frequently live underground or in dense vegetation. Whatever their size, however, all members of this order are

The Brazilian porcupine is adapted for its arboreal life. (AM)

united by their distinctive teeth – in particular a pair of large, chisel-like incisors that are constantly eroded to maintain a blade-like edge. These versatile tools can cut grass, pry open nuts, dig tunnels and gnaw anything worth gnawing; the word 'rodent' comes from the Latin *rodere*, which means 'to gnaw'. Rabbits and hares are not rodents but belong in the separate order Lagomorpha. The Pantanal is home to just one species.

LARGE ARBOREAL RODENTS

In the trees, keep an eye out for two large, arboreal rodents with long but very different tails. The bushy-tailed form of the Southern Amazon red squirrel (*Sciurus spadiceus*; family Sciuridae) will be familiar to visitors from North America and Europe. Active by day and a fan of palm nuts, its range only just reaches the Pantanal. The Brazilian porcupine (*Coendou prehensilis*; family Erethizontidae) is adapted for life among trees. Its feet have two modifications for grasping vines: a movable pad instead of a thumb, and a broad-soled hind foot. More noticeably, it has a muscular, prehensile tail that can spiral backwards to grip a branch. Porcupines are best known for the way in which they roll themselves into a ball as a defence strategy against predators, leaving only their barbed spines visible. One touch can leave these spines embedded in the aggressor's paw or muzzle, causing pain, at the very least, and sometimes more serious damage.

CAVY-LIKE RODENTS

Given their large size, hefty heads and tiny tails, you would be forgiven for thinking that the four rodents that make up this group were ungulates rather than rodents. Top of the list – in terms of size, abundance and entertainment value – is the capybara (*Hydrochaeris hydrochaeris*). This peccary-sized rodent is the world's largest, troubling the scales at a portly 50kg, and its squared-off muzzle and tiny eyes lend it a characteristic 'tough guy' demeanour. Capybaras are always in or near water, loafing on sandbanks or chomping on aquatic vegetation. They swim well, aided by partly webbed feet, and can hold their breath underwater for several minutes – useful skills if a jaguar is patrolling the riverside.

Active mainly by day, capybaras are sociable, living in family groups of up to six animals or in larger herds during the dry season.

Capybaras readily munch on water hyacinth. (JL)

The Brazilian guinea-pig (*Cavia aperea*) resembles a small capybara – and for good reason, as both are housed in the family Caviidae. Unlike its larger cousin, the guinea-pig (sometimes called a cavy) shuns water, grazing in short dry grassland but always within dashing distance of the dense vegetation that is criss-crossed with its runs.

A scuffling in the forest undergrowth may lead you to the region's sole representatives of the Cuniculidae and Dasyproctidae. The lowland paca (*Cuniculus paca*) belongs in the former family and is nocturnal, easily identified by its distinctive lines of white spots on chestnut flanks. Pair members share a territory but forage and den separately. Azara's agouti (*Dasyprocta azarae*) belongs in the Dasyproctidae and is, by contrast, a diurnal rodent

Capybara litter size ranges from one to seven. (JL)

Three superficially similar Pantanal rodents are Azara's agouti *(left, JL)*, Brazilian guinea-pig *(right, JL)* and lowland paca *(below, HP)*, but look for the paca's distinctive flank spots.

with a grizzled grey-brown and ginger coat. So little is known about this species that conservationists classify it as 'Data Deficient'. However, it is known to be a good planner, secreting fruit and nuts in subterranean caches to plunder during meagre times. It is also much easier to see than the paca.

MOUSE-LIKE RODENTS

Pity mammologists who specialise in the smaller end of the rodent spectrum. Theories on species limits and nomenclature in the New World's mouse-like rodents (Cricetidae) change every year, so rarely is there agreement on how many species are in the Pantanal – or even what they are called. Nevertheless, for the discerning visitor with an enquiring mind, these are fascinating mammals – not least for the variety of morphological adaptations with which evolutionary radiation has endowed the group.

Rice rats that live in trees, such as the unicoloured oecomys (*Oecomys concolor*), have broad feet with sharp curved claws, long tails and dense whiskers. Rodents that graze on the ground, such as the toba akodont (*Akodon toba*) and other grass mice, have fine whiskers and short tails; these mice also have long claws for digging tunnels under leaf litter. Terrestrial omnivores such as the elegant oryzomys (*Oryzomys nitidus*) have pointed snouts and large ears, so as to better detect insect prey. If disturbed, they often jump away to safety. The Chacoan marsh rat (*Holochilus chacarius*) is largely aquatic, so has partly webbed hind feet and dense, water-resistant fur. And if these diverse rodents don't tickle your fancy, there's always the roof or black rat (*Rattus rattus*), the ubiquitous scavenger transported to the New World on European ships several hundred years ago.

RABBIT

Bounding along with strong kicks of its long hind legs, the tapeti or Brazilian rabbit (*Sylvilagus brasiliensis*) is a frequent nocturnal sight in the Pantanal. A small cottontail in the family Leporidae, this species has the long ears, large eyes and short, furred tail that visitors associate with 'their' rabbits in the northern hemisphere. It is most active shortly after dusk and before dawn and has a taste for salt (including in dried human urine) as well as grass. If you succumbed to a call of nature during the day, it pays to return to the site shortly after nightfall!

A young tapeti or Brazilian rabbit. (HP)

MARSUPIALS

Opossums (family Didelphidae) are the sole Pantanal representatives of the marsupials, a group that has changed little since its evolution 65 million years ago. They are small to medium-sized mammals that recall rodents (order Rodentidae) with their pointed snouts, short legs, long tails and short fur.

Like other marsupials, opossums are famous for parental care. Opossum young are born tiny (1cm long and 0.5g in weight) and quickly ascend their mother's body to a nipple, where they remain attached for several weeks. Thereafter, some species (such as those in the genera *Didelphis* and *Philander*) protect their offspring in a pouch ('marsupium');

Look for white-eared opossums on the forest edge or near water. (JL)

others carry young on their back or leave them in a nest of dead leaves while they forage elsewhere. Most opossums are nocturnal and arboreal omnivores, consuming anything they come across.

At least seven species occur in the Pantanal. *Didelphis* opossums are the largest New World marsupials, measuring up to 1m, including tail. The common opossum (*D. marsupalis*) uses its bulk to tackle snakes and small animals, although also sips nectar in the dry season. A close encounter may be rather smelly: this opossum rolls in dung and readily squirts stinking urine. The white-eared opossum (*Didelphis albiventris*) differs by its white ears and black stripes on a white head. It is most often seen on the forest edge or near water. Both species are solitary, sexes meeting only to mate.

The grey four-eyed opossum (*Philander opossum*) is slightly smaller than *Didelphis* and easy to identify, with a large pale spot above each eye (hence the name). A voracious breeder, animals are sexually mature at seven months. The brown four-eyed opossum (*Metachirus nudicaudatus*) has dark ears and a largely hairless tail. Its stocky hind limbs are an adaptation to a terrestrial life. Seeing this marsupial requires stealth as, unlike other opossums, it flees at the slightest noise.

Gracile opossums (*Gracilinanus*), part of a wider grouping generally known as 'mouse opossums', are small pouchless marsupials with a prehensile tail much longer than their body. Just one species – the agile gracile opossum (*Gracilinanus agilis*) – occurs in the Pantanal, where it prefers the understorey of gallery forests. Dangling from a branch by its prehensile-tipped tail, this mouse-sized animal freezes in the torchlight before resuming feeding. Black eye-rings accentuate its huge eyes.

BIRDS

Southern crested caracaras are scavengers, constantly on the lookout for leftovers. (JL)

ven if birds have not previously been your thing, they certainly will be after your
Pantanal trip. The place is heaving with them – and many are large, colourful,
entertaining and confiding. Each habitat holds a different bird community, so you
should keep an eye out and an ear open wherever you are. At least 470 species have been
recorded (an oft-cited figure of 650 refers to a wider area), and birders easily rack up 130
in a day. The experts' 24-hour record is 196, but this is roughly the total that mere mortals
might see in a typical four-night stay.

GROUND BIRDS

Three unrelated families stride or shuffle across the Pantanal's dry terrain. Two are
entirely terrestrial and one is even flightless.

The flightless greater rhea is the tallest bird in the Americas. (JL)

RHEA

Standing taller than many *pantaneiros*, greater rheas (*Rhea americana*) are to Pantanal
grasslands what ostriches (*Struthio* sp.) are to African savannas. At 1.5m in height and 35kg
in weight, this is South America's largest bird. Although long-legged, long-necked and
flightless, dowdy plumage makes rheas remarkably tricky to spot. And once aware they
have been detected, they use those lanky limbs to race for the horizon. Males are
promiscuous, mating with many females. Unlike most polygamous birds, however, females

Look for red-winged tinamous peering warily out of tall grass. (JL)

lay eggs in a single nest that is attended solely by the male. The huge eggs weigh 600g – the equivalent of 12 chicken eggs. The male takes full responsibility for incubating the clutch and raising up to 30 young.

TINAMOUS

As you walk through Pantanal forests, a haunting voice may stop you in your tracks as it pierces the background hum. The mournful three-note whistle emanates from an undulated tinamou (*Crypturellus undulatus*), a member of the terrestrial, partridge-like Tinamidae. Tinamous are short-legged and short-tailed, but also long-necked and slender-billed. They lay arguably the most beautiful eggs in the world, so shiny that they resemble porcelain. Tinamous' brown or beige plumage assists in concealment: in grasslands, you may nearly tread on a red-winged tinamou (*Rhynchotus rufescens*) or spotted nothura (*Nothura maculosa*), which freeze upon feeling threatened and only flee, wings whirring, at the last second.

SERIEMA

The red-legged seriema (*Cariama cristata*) reinforces the impression of the African savannas, recalling a secretarybird (*Sagittarius serpentarius*) as it strides majestically across grasslands. This tall, leggy bird can run at 60km/h and rarely takes to the air. *Pantaneiros* like seriemas because they eat snakes. Their faintly menacing air derives from a staring eye and stiff, forward-pointing crest – but this is also one of very few birds with eyelashes.

The call of a territorial red-legged seriema carries a great distance. (BL)

Rufescent tiger-heron, scratching. (JL)

WATERBIRDS

As the world's largest wetland, it is unsurprising that the Pantanal is famous for its waterbirds. Among familiar families are herons, ducks and waders, while more exotic representatives include ibises and screamers. Dense congregations of feeding and nesting waterbirds provide unforgettable sights.

HERONS

Most herons (Ardeidae) saunter elegantly through the water before seizing a fish or frog with their dagger-shaped bill. More than a dozen species occur, many breeding in large, noisy treetop colonies. The compact striated heron (*Butorides striata*) calls stridently as it flies between riverbanks, where it adopts a rail-like crouch before pouncing on an unsuspecting fish. The rufescent tiger-heron (*Tigrisoma lineatum*) lives up to its name by starting life in tiger-striped plumage; juveniles take two years to assume the adult's distinguished rufous and grey garb. Alongside the lanky cocoi heron (*Ardea cocoi*) and suave little blue heron (*Egretta caerulea*), look for snowy egret (*E. thula*) and cattle egret (*Bubuculus ibis*). The latter is a familiar Old World species that crossed the Atlantic of its own accord and subsequently colonised the Americas.

A striated heron crouches while hunting. (JL)

Three herons are primarily nocturnal. Of these, the black-crowned night-heron (*Nycticorax nycticorax*) is the most common and also frequently feeds by day. Amazingly similar in plumage – but only distantly related – is the boat-billed heron (*Cochlearius cochlearius*). Its bill shape is astonishing, being extremely wide and flat, with the upper mandible shaped like an inverted boat keel (see page 126). The diminutive zigzag heron (*Zebrilus undulatus*) is a predominantly Amazonian species that has been discovered recently in dense riparian vegetation in Mato Grosso.

The final trio of herons vie to be beauty queen. The whistling heron (*Syrigma sibilatrix*) is attired in pinkish-yellow and powder blue (see page 95), with long head plumes and a bright pink bill-base. Its unique whistling call attracts attention when in flight. The capped heron (*Pilherodius pileatus*) has a subtler appearance, but its sublime cream plumage and cyan bill are breathtaking. Arguably the most stunning family member, however, and certainly the most sought after, is the agami heron (*Agamia agami*). Sticking to shady riverbanks, this shy heron shimmers chestnut and pale blue when it catches the light.

A flying great egret is all wings and legs. (JL)

The agami heron is arguably the Pantanal's most beautiful waterbird. (OP)

IBISES AND SPOONBILLS

Ibises (Threskiornithidae) represent an evolutionary link between herons and storks, and are a prominent feature of the Pantanal. Visitors are most likely to see the plumbeous ibis (*Theristictus caerulescens*), buff-necked ibis (*T. caudatus*) and green ibis (*Mesembrinibis cayennensis*). While most ibises breed in colonies, like herons, these three nest alone, like storks. The delicate plumbeous ibis (see page 131) sifts its downcurved bill through shallow water, neck ruffle rippling in the breeze. The

The green ibis is less secretive in the Pantanal than elsewhere. (JL)

buff-necked ibis is a noisier proposition, pairs broadcasting their arrival to all and sundry. Most intriguing is the green ibis. A secretive forest denizen elsewhere in its range, this small ibis loses its inhibitions here, feeding in the open, far from trees. In the sunlight, its wings and neck glint green and blue, bringing a superficially dowdy bird to life.

A flash of pink announces the arrival of a pair of roseate spoonbills. (CdJ)

Dowdy is not an adjective applicable to roseate spoonbills (*Platalea ajaja*). Even a hardened birder obsessed with plumage minutiae on little brown jobs cannot fail to be captivated by these flamingo-pink birds swishing their bills through the water, straining it for aquatic insects and small fish. Long, straight and flat, the spoonbill's bill broadens to a bulbous tip that gives the bird its name.

STORKS

Enormous nests – constructed from thick, metre-long branches – enthroning isolated tall trees can only mean one thing: we are in jabiru (*Jabiru mycteria*) territory. With a wingspan of 2.5m, the jabiru is the giant of the Pantanal skies, into which it rises on thermals before soaring to distant feeding grounds. When this enormous bird is excited or stressed, its inflatable throat sac fills with blood and turns vibrant scarlet. Jabirus differ from the two other Pantanal storks (Ciconiidae) in feeding behaviour; each species occupies its own niche in the wetland ecosystem. The jabiru bounces energetically, plunging its bill into the water to terrify hidden fish into the open. The bald-headed wood stork (*Mycteria americana*) forages more calmly, using its feet to stir up sediment and seizing any creature that brushes the sensitive tip of its immersed bill. Maguari storks (*Ciconia maguari*), red-faced and white-eyed, lurk in tall marshy vegetation, hunting by sight rather than touch.

An adult jabiru, preening. (JL)

Wood storks, the most gregarious of the Pantanal's storks, wade through wetlands in search of food. (MU)

Anhinga swallowing a fish. (JL)

CORMORANT AND ANHINGA

An accomplished diver, the Neotropic cormorant (*Phalacrocorax brasilianus*) dries itself by extending its wings, allowing air to circulate and sun to warm. The anhinga (*Anhinga anhinga*) behaves identically, despite belonging in a separate family (Anhingidae). With its sinuous neck and long, fine bill, this attenuated bird resembles a cormorant that has been stretched on a rack. When swimming, with just its neck protruding above the surface, it resembles an altogether different creature, hence its colloquial name of 'snakebird'. The anhinga uses its bill to spear fish underwater. Then, raising head and fish above the surface, it tosses up the catch and swallows it in a single gulp.

WILDFOWL AND SCREAMERS

A first-time Pantanal visitor might expect the world's largest wetlands to be heaving with wildfowl (Anatidae). Yet the opposite is true: ducks are notable for their scarcity. Only a dozen species occur – and patchily at that. Three species of whistling-duck (*Dendrocygna*) consort in large, mixed flocks. Whistling-ducks are named after the melodious calls of two of the trio. The other common duck may look vaguely familiar: muscovy ducks (*Cairina*

On the wing, the southern screamer is almost eagle-like. (JL)

moschata) have been domesticated for more than 2,000 years and their varied descendants waddle across farmyards worldwide.

Given that their voice carries 3km, you will probably hear screamers (Anhimidae) before you see them. The deep, loud calls are alternately melodious and screechy, so the bird is well named. You may also discern two voices, for screamer pairs duet. Two species inhabit the Pantanal, although the horned screamer (*Anhima cornuta*) occurs only sparsely in Mato Grosso. You are more likely to encounter southern screamers (*Chauna torquata*), long-legged turkey-like birds on the ground that mutate into massive, eagle-like creatures in stately flight. Neither simile would lead you to believe that the screamers' nearest relatives are actually wildfowl.

Grey-necked wood-rails hunt stealthily in muddy water. (JL)

RAILS, GALLINULES AND JACANA

Rails, crakes and gallinules (Rallidae) generally skulk in dense marshy vegetation. Nine species range from the lark-sized rufous-sided crake (*Laterallus melanophaius*) to the duck-sized purple gallinule (*Porphyrio martinica*) and grey-necked wood-rail (*Aramides cajanea*). The wood-rail and gallinule are the easiest to see: the former is lanky and loud-voiced; the latter lumbering and bright-coloured. Recalling gallinules but unrelated to them, the wattled jacana (*Jacana jacana*) is a firm favourite among visitors. The attraction lies in its gawky gait and fascinating family life. The jacana's absurdly long legs and toes are adaptations to a life spent teetering on floating vegetation, a habit that prompts the colloquial name of 'lily-trotter'. Jacanas are among just 1% of birds that practise polyandry, a breeding system where the female mates with several males that each assume responsibility for parental care. A male's duties include fleeing danger with chicks lodged under his wings, only their dangling legs visible.

Crouched heron-like, the sunbittern is a mass of stripes. (JL)

SUNBITTERN, SUNGREBE AND LIMPKIN

This trio of unrelated birds is taxonomically fascinating. The sungrebe (*Heliornis fulica*) is the sole New World representative of a family (Heliornithidae) that also has single members in Africa and Asia. The other two – the sunbittern (*Eurypyga helias*) and limpkin (*Aramus guarauna*) – have an even greater claim to taxonomic uniqueness: each is the only member of its family and has no close relatives.

Swimming furtively near a shady riverbank, a sungrebe resembles a flattened duck. This wary bird hides in vegetation or flees on long wings and drooping tail. Visitors often see a

Like the sunbittern (*top*), the limpkin is taxonomically unique. (JL)

sungrebe along the same stretch of river as a sunbittern. At first glance, the latter bird resembles a stripy heron, with long legs, sinuous neck and sharply pointed bill. It even behaves like a hyperactive egret, striding along the shore before snaring an unsuspecting crab. While immaculately camouflaged at rest, however, the sunbittern is simply dazzling when opening its wings in threat or flight. The flight feathers sport a startling pattern of chestnut, yellow and black, which suggests a pair of huge staring eyes and is enough to make any predator think twice. The limpkin is no less distinctive. Taking its name from its hobbling walk, this bird has a twisted windpipe that amplifies its call. In flight – with deep, elastic wing beats – a limpkin is unlike any other bird. And its sharp, jinked bill-tip is the perfect tool for hammering open its principal prey, aquatic apple snails (*Pomacea guyanensis*).

WADERS

Of a score of waders spread across three families, four are resident while others migrate to South America from northern hemisphere breeding grounds. The quartet comprises two lapwings, a plover and a stilt. The beautiful pied lapwing (*Vanellus cayanus*), elegantly patterned with black, white and brown, breeds on sandy beaches flanking rivers. This habitat, or a simple

Pied lapwing, a riverside treat. (AM)

muddy shore, also attracts the collared plover (*Charadrius collaris*), which delights in sprinting long distances. The southern lapwing (*Vanellus chilensis*) is ubiquitous. Noisy and crested, it shrieks in alarm whenever it spots a potential predator, making it a favourite of *pantaneiros* guarding livestock. Black-necked stilts (*Himantopus mexicanus*) wade delicately through water on elongated limbs. Among visiting waders, white-rumped sandpipers (*Calidris fuscicollis*) swarm along lakeshores while groups of lesser yellowlegs (*Tringa flavipes*) loaf in knee-deep shallows. Unlike these sociable creatures, the aptly named solitary sandpiper (*T. solitaria*) prefers its own company on a secluded muddy pool.

The black skimmer furrows the water surface with its lower mandible. (JL)

TERNS AND SKIMMERS

Terns (Sternidae) are a feature of any river trip. South America's joint-smallest species – yellow-billed tern (*Sternula superciliaris*) – often sits alongside one of the biggest, the large-billed tern (*Phaetusa simplex*). Both breed on river beaches, often near black skimmers (*Rynchops niger*), a tern-like member of a different family (Rynchopidae). Skimmers have remarkable bills, the lower mandible being half as long again as the upper. They hunt by flying low over the water, lower mandible furrowing the surface. When one senses a small fish, it dips its head and scoops up the prize.

Snail kite, with its distinctive, sharply hooked bill (JL)

RAPTORS

Few birds evoke more immediate awe than raptors (or birds of prey). With sharp eyesight, powerful talons and malevolent hooked bills, these imposing predators sit regally atop the avian food chain. Forty species have been seen in the Pantanal, but many are rare, so a good haul would be a third of these.

KITES, HARRIER AND OSPREY

Floating languidly low over roadside wetlands, a snail kite (*Rostrhamus sociabilis*) quickly catches the visitor's eye. Its narrow, sharply hooked bill provides a deft tool with which to prise apple snails from their shells. Other kites (Accipitridae) hunt higher above ground. About 30m up, a white-tailed kite (*Elanus leucurus*) hovers delicately on long, upraised wings, scrutinising ground vegetation for an oblivious rodent. The exquisite pearl kite (*Gampsonyx swainsonii*) soars at great heights, its beauty only apparent when it descends to a tree. Plumbeous kites (*Ictinia plumbea*) and swallow-tailed kites (*Elanoides forficatus*) congregate in graceful flocks to feed on winged termites.

Like snail kites, male and female long-winged harriers (*Circus buffoni*) differ markedly in plumage; they quarter grasslands, seeking frogs and rodents. Ospreys (*Pandion haliaetus*), by contrast, dive at 80km/h to catch fish that venture too close to the surface. One of the front talons is reversible, so the osprey moves it backwards to help grab its prey.

The savanna hawk captures small animals on the ground. (JL)

HAWKS AND EAGLES

Pantanal hawks and eagles (also Accipitridae) are an eclectic bunch. They vary from true hawks (genus *Accipiter*) through buzzard-type birds (*Buteo*) to the massive crested eagle (*Morphnus guianensis*). Along the way are oddities such as the crane hawk (*Geranospiza caerulescens*), which uses extremely long legs and short outer toes to reach into tree cavities, and the black-chested buzzard-eagle (*Geranoaetus melanoleucus*), whose short tail is barely visible beyond its immensely broad wings.

Black-collared hawks loiter on riversides before pouncing on discarded fish. (CdJ)

The commonest species are the black-collared hawk (*Busarellus nigricollis*) and savanna hawk (*Buteogallus meridionalis*). The latter waits near burning vegetation in order to capture small animals disorientated by smoke, and nabs subterranean blind snakes (*Typhlops*) that emerge above ground during rain. Black-collared hawks are permanent fixtures along rivers, their fish-catching abilities enhanced by long claws and spiny undersides to the toes. Some individuals have learnt to associate humans with fish; they loiter in riverside trees, waiting for discarded catches. Also seen along rivers, but particularly in marshy areas near forest, is the great black-hawk (*Buteogllus urubitinga*), which has a taste for venomous snakes.

The roadside hawk (*Buteo magnirostris*) is the smallest of three buzzard-like species. It scans for movement from a prominent vantage point, before flying with a distinctive action that alternates rapid flaps and long glides. The white-tailed hawk (*B. albicaudatus*) is one of several raptors that comes in two plumage varieties, including a confusing dark phase. The zone-tailed hawk (*B. albonotatus*) is consistently dark-plumaged – and for good reason. This remarkable raptor imitates a vulture (*Cathartes*) in coloration, wing shape and flight style. It thus lulls small birds and mammals into a false sense of security, as they believe it to be a vulture and thus incapable of attacking live prey.

Although they prefer snakes, great black-hawks are also accomplished fishers. (JL)

A male American kestrel. (JL)

FALCONS AND CARACARAS

Members of the Falconidae differ markedly in form and function. At the 'classic' end of the spectrum are four true falcons – dashing, aerodynamic hunters that pursue small birds and insects in rapid flight. The most common are the American kestrel (*Falco sparverius*) and bat falcon (*F. rufigularis*). The latter targets bats as they emerge from their roost at dusk – though during daylight it happily hunts dragonflies and other aerial insects. Forest-falcons are larger. Two species – collared (*Micrastur semitorquatus*) and barred (*M. ruficollis*) – are more often heard (at dawn) than seen. Known for its chortling call, the laughing falcon (*Herpetotheres cachinnans*) is revered among *pantaneiros* for its snake-catching abilities. Caracaras are generalist omnivores, nibbling fruit and digesting carrion. The dapper yellow-headed caracara (*Milvago chimachima*) perches on livestock, picking botflies off their backs and snatching insects disturbed by their hooves. The southern crested caracara (*Polyborus plancus*) is a brute. With massive bill, shaggy crest and long legs, it bounds along the ground, chicken-like. Its bare face changes colour from red to yellow with excitement.

✓ VULTURES

New World vultures (Cathartidae), unlike those of the Old World (Accipitridae), are not related to raptors but to storks, with which they share a near-identical foot structure. Vultures perform an essential ecological role by consuming decaying flesh and are

Black vultures scavenge dead flesh, even from a yacaré caiman. (JL)

immune to the botulism that would afflict a human scavenger. Bare heads render these birds ugly but perform a useful function, preventing decomposing animal matter from contaminating the plumage. The Pantanal's vulture quartet falls into two distinct groups, divided by whether they locate dead animals by sight or smell. The stunning king vulture (*Sacoramphus papa*) and reptilian black vulture (*Corygyps atrata*) soar high, using acute vision to spot their next meal: even 3,000m up, they can spot a corpse just 30cm long. In contrast, the turkey vulture (*Cathartes aura*) and lesser yellow-headed vulture (*C. burrovianus*) have exceptional olfactory powers so quarter low above trees, sniffing for a concealed carcass.

GUANS

Guans, chacalacas and curassows (Cracidae) resemble arboreal pheasants. All are very large birds with long legs, neck and tail sticking out from a bulky body. You have a good chance of seeing four or five species in the Pantanal. Indeed, there is little chance of missing the Chaco chacalaca (*Ortalis canicollis*), an avian alarm clock with a pre-dawn song that reverberates for over 2km – far enough to incite a neighbouring group to respond.

Piping-guans display a fleshy dewlap of a throat sac that droops below the bill. The colour of this wattle helps birders distinguish between red-throated (*Pipile cujubi*) and blue-throated piping-guans (*P. cumanensis*) – although, confusingly, the dewlap of the Pantanal blue-throated is often white! To further complicate matters, the Pantanal is a hybridisation zone, so it is anyone's guess where best to draw taxonomic limits. Little wonder that some ornithologists lump the forms as a single species. Rather than struggle with identification challenges, then, far better simply to relax and enjoy the piping-guans' instrumental music. As the male display-glides between treetops, the movement of air through his outermost wing feathers – which narrow abruptly towards their tip – produces an explosive ripping sound rather like machine-gun fire.

Bare-faced curassow (*above*) and Chaco chacalaca (*below*) are the most frequently seen cracids. (JL)

The two other members of this family are no less remarkable. The globally threatened chestnut-bellied guan (*Penelope ochrogaster*) has such a tiny distribution that the Transpantaneira is almost the only place to see it. Bare-faced curassows (*Crax fasciolata*) top the cracid beauty stakes – doubly so because male and female differ so markedly in plumage that they resemble separate species. The male's black garb fuses with forest shadows, so you may need binoculars to discern his curly crest feathers. The female has similar headgear but is far easier to see, being tiger-striped above.

PARROTS AND THEIR ALLIES

Few bird families are as closely associated with humans as the Psittacidae, which comprises macaws, parakeets, parrots and parrotlets. Their cultural importance needs little introduction, as parrots embed themselves in human life as pets, status symbols, meat and sartorial adornments. A score of parrots and their allies inhabit the Pantanal, of which the average visitor may easily see half.

HYACINTH MACAW

A raucous roar announces the arrival of a hyacinth macaw (*Anodorhynchus hyacinthinus*), the Pantanal bird that all visitors want to see. Measuring a full metre in length and hitting the scales at a hefty 1.5kg, this is the world's largest parrot. It is also one of the rarest, its population having crashed as a result of habitat destruction and illegal trapping for the cage-bird trade. Just 6,500 birds are thought to remain in Brazil, eastern Bolivia and northern Paraguay. This compares with an estimated 10,000 birds captured for trade during the 1980s.

As if this combination of size and scarcity were not sufficient to whet the appetite of even the least bird-orientated of tourists, the hyacinth macaw is also breathtakingly beautiful. Rich cobalt-blue plumage is offset by bare yellow skin around eye and bill (see page 13). The result is a clown-like grin, an impression exacerbated by the macaw's jaunty demeanour and clumsy movements as it waddles along the ground or uses its bill to clamber around a tree.

With their demonstrative behaviour and jaunty demeanour, hyacinth macaws are crowd-pleasers. (JL)

The main function of the huge bill, however, is as a powerful nutcracker. The hyacinth macaw's diet largely comprises the hard fruit of a handful of palm trees, particularly the *acuri* and *bocaiúva*. Its preference for these nutritious fruits is one reason for its relative abundance in the Pantanal, now home to three-quarters of the entire population. Another is the success of recent conservation projects, some motivated by a growing realisation that the macaw is an economic asset that draws tourists to the region.

Most tourist *fazendas* host breeding hyacinth macaws. In many cases, pairs breed within metres of the lodge, years without human persecution leading Pantanal macaws to perceive man as friend rather than foe. Such a circle of trust benefits the visitor, who can enjoy scintillating views while sipping a beer. Like all the Pantanal's parrots bar one, the hyacinth macaw is a cavity-nester. While preferring natural holes in tall trees, particularly the *manduvi*, it readily takes advantage of large nestboxes erected specifically for its use. Most pairs breed between July and December and are thus often incubating eggs or raising young during the main tourist season.

OTHER MACAWS

The other macaws are less easy to see. The smallest, and most common, is the yellow-collared macaw (*Primolius auricollis*). Mating for life, pairs mutually preen and canoodle. In reality it is a pseudo-macaw – in Portuguese, a *maracanã* rather than an *arara*. The two true *araras* are large and gaudy. The blue-and-yellow macaw (*Ara ararauna*) reaches the southern limit of its range in the Pantanal and has predominantly cyan and yellow plumage. The red-and-green macaw (*A. chloropterus*) is similarly named after its principal colours, but also displays large blue patches on wings and tail. You are most likely to see these impressive birds as they fly between feeding grounds.

PARAKEETS

In a family that routinely nests alone in tree cavities, the monk parakeet (*Myiopsitta monachus*) is the proverbial sore thumb. It is the only New World parrot to breed colonially and the only one to build its own, stick nest. Pairs cut twigs to add to the huge nest structure, in which they occupy a private chamber. Two other species, the peach-fronted parakeet (*Aratinga aurea*) and nanday parakeet (*Nandayus nenday*), often join monk parakeets

The white-eyed parakeet *(left, AG)* and nanday parakeet *(right, MU)* are among the more common Pantanal representatives of this colourful family.

in their unusual habit of foraging, dove-like, on the ground. The former is exquisite, with a subtle orange forehead, yellow eye-ring and blue flash on each wing. It is one of few members of this family to benefit from deforestation. Guttural cries from large flocks of nanday parakeet are a common Pantanal sound. Indeed, calls are the best way to identify parakeets as they zip overhead: large birds, such as white-eyed (*Aratinga leucophthalma*) and blue-crowned parakeets (*A. acuticaudata*), have deep, harsh vocalisations; flocks of the compact yellow-chevroned parakeet (*Brotogeris chiriri*) communicate with a shrill chirruping. Intermediate between these two genera in both size and call is the blaze-winged parakeet (*Pyrrhura devillei*), a speciality of Mato Grosso do Sul.

Blue-fronted parrot. (JL)

PARROTS AND PARROTLETS

The most conspicuous of the Pantanal's parrot quintet is also the largest: the blue-fronted parrot (*Amazona aestiva*). It allows close approach, this trusting nature perhaps the cause of its frequent domestication; blue-fronted parrots make excellent 'talkers'. Orange-winged parrots (*A. amazonica*) resemble their blue-fronted cousin, but instead of a cyan forehead have a yellow central crown stripe with cyan on either side. Scaly-headed parrots (*Pionus maximiliani*) are smaller and have a distinctive flight manner: whereas the heavy wingbeats of *Amazona* parrots recall ducks, and parakeets briefly close their wings between bouts of rapid flapping, the scaly-headed parrot's downstroke brings its wings vertically below the body. The blue-winged parrotlet (*Forpus xanthopterygius*) can be a devil to see well. This sparrow-sized parrot blends in with green vegetation when foraging on fruits then flees into the distance at the slightest sign of trouble.

TRAPPING AND TRADING

Humans have harvested and traded wild birds for thousands of years, whether for food, pets, culture or sport. In recent decades, however, the bird trade has burgeoned into a billion-dollar industry. Increasing demand, improved access, enhanced capture techniques and expanding air travel are pushing the exploitation of many species beyond sustainable levels. As a consequence, more than one-quarter of the world's bird species have been recorded in international trade, with millions of individuals changing hands each year. Worse still, one-tenth of birds threatened with global extinction are victims. Among Pantanal species – as in many parts of the world – parrots are the most susceptible, being prized both for their beauty and their ability to mimic humans. A third more hyacinth macaws were snared in Brazil during the 1980s than remain in the whole of South America today. Trade is big business, but local benefits are small. A local farmer sells a blue-fronted parrot to a local trader for US$4, just 1% of its final retail value. Songbirds are also highly prized: several species of seedeater (*Sporophila*) that migrate through the Pantanal each year risk extinction as a result of intense trapping pressure.

NEAR-PASSERINES

The term 'near-passerine' is a convenient – if technically controversial – catch-all for a disparate assemblage of bird groups that resemble the passerines (pages 78–88) in general appearance and behaviour, but differ in toe morphology. Parrots fall into this group, but are treated separately (above).

The distinctively plumaged scaled dove occurs in small groups in open areas. (JL)

PIGEONS AND DOVES

Most of the Pantanal's dozen members of this homogeneous family (Columbidae) feed on the ground, head bobbing as they scuttle along, picking up seeds or fallen fruits. Ruddy ground-doves (*Columbina talpacoti*) and eared doves (*Zenaida auriculata*) are regulars around bird tables and other human habitation. Less tame are the scaled dove (*C. squammata*), unique in its scaly appearance, and long-tailed ground-dove (*Uropelia campestris*). The latter occurs only in the savannas of central Brazil and east Bolivia, so the Pantanal is a great place to see it. With a surprisingly noisy take-off for such tiny birds, a skittish group of picui ground-doves (*C. picui*) escape danger on whirring wings.

A handful of larger columbids are associated with wooded habitats. The otherwise dull plumage of picazuro pigeons (*Patagioenas picazuro*) is relieved by a glossy, reflective neck-patch. Pale-vented pigeons (*P. cayennensis*) sing from an exposed perch – like other columbids, with the bill apparently closed. Two stocky doves in the genus *Leptotila* are hard to differentiate, and even expert birders usually pass. Both offer interesting insights into columbid behaviour: a nervous white-tipped dove (*L. verreauxi*) bobs its tail, while a courting grey-fronted dove (*L. rufiaxilla*) claps its wings while cooing softly.

With its beady eye, shaggy crest and baggy trousers, the guira cuckoo oozes personality. (JL)

CUCKOOS

Cuckoos (Cuculidae) are infamous for playing no part in parenthood other than laying their eggs in other species' nests. But this breeding strategy – brood parasitism – is actually deployed by only half of the world's cuckoos. The proportion in the New World tropics is even lower. Only two cuckoos breeding in the Pantanal do not raise their own young: the striped cuckoo (*Tapera naevia*) and pheasant cuckoo (*Dromococcyx phasianellus*). These parasites lay noticeably petite eggs

to match those of substantially smaller host species such as spinetails (*Synallaxis*). Getting a good view of either requires bags of patience: both sit motionless in dense vegetation, revealing their presence only by their simple whistling calls, repeated indefatigably for hours. More visible – although far from tame – are the squirrel cuckoo (*Piaya cayana*) and little cuckoo (*Coccycua minuta*). The former is large and long-tailed, with chestnut upperparts and largely pink underparts. While foraging for caterpillars, it manoeuvres through vegetation with a nimbleness that belies its size. The little cuckoo is a pint-sized version of the squirrel cuckoo; the latter's 'Mini-Me', perhaps.

These four cuckoos are solitary and furtive birds. The remaining trio are the opposite – gregarious and showy. Flocks of the scruffy, punk-like guira cuckoo (*Guira guira*) play 'follow-my-leader', birds taking turns to flutter a short distance before crashing into vegetation, apparently exhausted. Anis recall guira cuckoos in behaviour and shape, but have iridescent black plumage and deep-based, steeply arched bills. The greater ani (*Crotophaga major*) is the size of a squirrel cuckoo, equipped with a menacing white eye and invariably found in waterside trees. The appreciably smaller smooth-billed ani (*C. ani*) has less restrictive habitat requirements; visitors frequently enjoy close views of groups sitting on *fazenda* fences.

Tropical screech-owls come in two colour phases, which readily pair up. (OS)

OWLS

Owls (Strigidae/Tytonidae) are among the most widely recognised of all bird groups, in part because of the fearful fascination that we have with 'creatures of the night'. Thanks to excellent eyesight and superlative hearing, owls are to night what raptors are to day: consummate avian predators at the pinnacle of the food chain. Their nocturnal habits mean that you should head out at night to see more than a couple of the Pantanal's nine species.

Burrowing owls are active by day, perching prominently in savannas and other open areas. (JL)

By day, the tropical screech-owl (*Megascops choliba*) and great horned owl (*Bubo virginianus*) avoid detection through their nondescript plumage and elongated ear tufts. The tufts have nothing to do with hearing, but assist camouflage by resembling the tip of a broken vertical branch. Despite such tricks, small birds often spot the owl and blow its cover. They mob the predator until the owl grudgingly accepts that it must find peace elsewhere.

You have a greater chance of seeing the two smallest owls, as both are predominantly diurnal. The burrowing owl (*Athene cunicularia*) shuns forests in favour of open grasslands. It breeds in armadillo burrows, termite mounds or other terrestrial holes. The nesting pair widens the entrance hole and excavates a horizontal gallery that the two birds line with manure or dry grass. The ferruginous pygmy-owl (*Glaucidium brasilianum*) is barely sparrow-sized (see page 157), but has no qualms about tackling a victim as large as itself. Pygmy-owls fool prey with their false, 'occipital' face. On the back of the head, two black spots flanked by white lines give the impression of large eyes. An unsuspecting bird spots this 'face' and makes a beeline for the 'rear' of the owl, unwittingly entering the danger zone. Such is the fear that pygmy-owls generate among small birds that a whistled imitation of the owl's call may attract skulking passerines into view as they gang up on the perceived threat.

NIGHTJARS AND POTOOS

Nightjars (Caprimulgidae) are dove-sized birds that become active at dusk and characterise excursions on warm, dry nights. With narrow wings and long tails, they recall falcons as they hunt for aerial insects above forest, grassland or river. Huge eyes help them spot their prey –

The most frequently seen nightjar, common pauraques emerge onto roads at dusk. (JL)

and many species use bristles around the bill to funnel it into their wide mouths. By day, most nightjars roost on the ground or along horizontal branches, relying on complex plumage patterns to offer concealment from predators.

Of the ten species, you are most likely to see band-tailed nighthawks (*Nyctiprogne leucopyga*), large numbers of which hawk above rivers at dusk. Locally common around wetlands, nacunda nighthawks (*Podager nacunda*) are the Pantanal's largest nightjar. They are easily identified in flight by their broad wings, short tail and white underparts, but less distinctive when roosting on the ground, when they resemble a cowpat! In wooded areas, you might spot a scissor-tailed nightjar (*Hydropsalis torquata*) enjoying the residual warmth of a road. The male is dramatically attired; elongated tail feathers account for two-thirds of its length. When caught in headlights, the common pauraque (*Nyctidromus albicollis*) makes a short vertical leap before returning to the ground. It has longer legs than other nightjars, enabling it to walk rapidly.

A great potoo at rest by day looks uncannily like part of a tree. (JL)

Closely related to nightjars are potoos (*Nyctibiidae*). By day, both the great potoo (*Nyctibius grandis*) and common potoo (*N. griseus*) roost erect on tree stumps, mimicking a broken-off branch with their camouflaged plumage. These wonderful creatures have 'magic eyes': the upper eyelid has two incisions that enable the bird to keep a lookout even with its eyes closed. Never has an immobile bird been so interesting! Potoos come to life after dusk when they hawk insects from an exposed perch. At full moon, the common potoo's melancholic wail is a characteristic sound of the Pantanal.

HUMMINGBIRDS

The burst of glittering green is gone even quicker than it arrived, leaving the observer to wonder whether the mind is playing tricks. Such is a typical first encounter with a hummingbird, a beautiful and extravagant family (Trochilidae) exclusive to the Americas. Hummingbirds are jewels of the avian world, their names embodying precious stones such as amethyst, emerald, sapphire and topaz. They are also birds of extremes. One tiny species, the amethyst woodstar (*Calliphlox amethystina*), weighs just 2.5g, while even the black-throated mango (*Anthracothorax nigricollis*), one of the larger species, barely troubles the scales at 6.5g. A hummingbird's heart is relatively larger than that of any other bird, beating 1,000 times per minute to pump oxygen and nutrients around the body. A fast metabolism goes hand in hand with hyperactivity: hummingbirds fly at great speed, wings flapping up to 80 times per second.

'Hummers' are an enthralling part of the Pantanal experience. Sit quietly near a flowering plant and prepare to be entranced as hummingbirds hover by the blooms,

Flying jewels: female glittering-bellied emerald (*left*) and male black-throated mango (*right*). (JL)

inserting their bill to extract nectar. Common species around lodge gardens include glittering-bellied emerald (*Chlorostilbon aureoventris*), versicoloured emerald (*Amazilia versicolor*) and gilded sapphire (*Hylocharis chrysura*). With luck, you may be graced with a visit from a larger species such as planalto hermit (*Phaethornis pretrei*), elongated central tail feathers dangling, or white-tailed goldenthroat (*Polytmus guainumbi*).

Alternatively, visit flowering trees in the forest – the domain of the fork-tailed woodnymph (*Thalurania furcata*), the male a shimmering blue. Males of some hummingbirds, such as the localised cinnamon-throated hermit (*Phaethornis nattereri*), congregate in a single place, called a 'lek', to sing and display to females. In the southern Pantanal, you may see the spectacular swallow-tailed hummingbird (*Eupetomena macroura*); pairs zigzag into the air in display.

Blue-crowned motmots gleam in the forest gloom. (HP)

TROGONS, MOTMOTS AND JACAMARS

Amidst the forest gloom, the visitor's eye is drawn to a long-tailed bird sat serenely on a horizontal branch. It could equally be a trogon (family Trogonidae), jacamar (Gabulidae) or motmot (Motmotidae), a distantly related suite of vibrantly coloured birds. A quick look at the bill clarifies the family: a trogon's is short and stubby; a jacamar's is long and fine-tipped (prompting its local name of 'needlebill'); and a motmot's lies in between, being downcurved and of moderate length. Of the two trogons, you are most likely to see the blue-crowned (*Trogon curucui*), which has a blue-green sheen to the head and bright red underparts. Rufous-tailed jacamars (*Galbula*

73

ruficauda) are common and allow close approach as they pose calmly between bouts of flycatching. This beautiful bird (see page 6) shimmers green above and glows rufous below. The most distinctive feature of the blue-crowned motmot (*Momotus momota*) is its tail, which it shows off by swinging sideways: the two elongated, central tail feathers have a bare shaft and terminate in a vivid blue spatula. Motmots excavate nest burrows in sandy banks – a habit shared with their nearest relatives, kingfishers.

Amazon kingfishers can be found along most watercourses. (JL)

A ringed kingfisher carries away its fishy prey. (JL)

KINGFISHERS

A sudden splash in the river and a jade bird zooms to an isolated branch, fish clasped in bill. The Pantanal is blessed with all of South America's five resident kingfishers (Alcedinidae), and many visitors are goggle-eyed at their hunting exploits. All employ an identical fishing strategy: sit, watch, wait and dive. But they are far from identical in size. The largest and most common species, the ringed kingfisher (*Megaceryle torquata*), is 20 times heavier than the tiniest and rarest, the American pygmy kingfisher (*Chloroceryle aenea*).

Erect-crested and conspicuous, the ringed kingfisher demands attention as it perches on roadside telegraph wires or other vantage points above a watercourse. Only the female exhibits the grey chest band encapsulated in the name. Two-thirds the size, the male Amazon kingfisher (*Chloroceryle amazona*) differs from the female in its chestnut breast band. Near-identical in plumage, but another degree smaller, is the green kingfisher (*C. americana*), which appears chequered in flight due to the white spots on its flight feathers. Roughly the same size is the reclusive green-and-rufous kingfisher (*C. inda*), which has dark green upperparts and warm cinnamon underparts. Together with the similar-plumaged but even smaller American pygmy kingfisher, this species favours dense riverine vegetation along small streams.

TOUCANS AND PUFFBIRDS

Sailing between forest canopy and fruiting tree on wings that alternately flap frantically and glide languorously, the toco toucan (*Ramphastos toco*) would make an incongruous sight even without its outsized banana of a bill. This massive appendage provokes both astonishment and mirth in the first-time observer who may only know the bird from tourism adverts or television commercials. Scientists now believe that the bill helps the toucan regulate its body temperature by effectively sucking out excess heat from the body. Toco toucans regularly visit fruiting trees, where they move restlessly, tail cocked, before plucking a choice morsel with surprising deftness. Tocos also have carnivorous tendencies, and groups ransack the hanging

Its huge bill poses no barrier to this toco toucan's dextrous consumption of tiny fruit. (JL)

nests of yellow-rumped cacique colonies (see page 88) or investigate tree holes to extract parrot eggs.

The other common toucan (Toucanidae) is the chestnut-eared aracari (*Pteroglossus castanotis*). Smaller and more gregarious than the toco, aracaris often bicker in a fruiting tree or buzz between feeding areas in fast, direct flight. This colourful species has a strongly patterned bill, yellow and chestnut underparts, and staring white eye. You may

Chestnut-eared aracaris are gregarious toucans unafraid to venture close to human habitation. (OP)

A striking red bill relieves the sombre plumage of the black-fronted nunbird. (JL)

need a close look to pick out the brownish sides to the face that give the bird its English name.

Perched motionless for long periods and cryptically garbed, puffbirds (Bucconidae) can be hard to spot in dry, open-country vegetation as they wait for a lizard to break cover. At the end of their large heads, both white-eared puffbird (*Nystalus chacaru*) and spot-backed puffbird (*N. maculatus*) have powerful, hook-tipped red bills: the perfect tool for dismantling reptiles. Sun-worshipping puffbirds are absent from forest, replaced by black-fronted nunbirds (*Monasa nigrifrons*). The shade-loving nunbird's bill and behaviour resemble those of the puffbirds, but its plumage is a uniform smoky-black. Like the puffbirds, the nunbird is fearless and allows close approach.

FRIEND OR FOE?

You might think it logical for birds to have an innate hatred of predators that steal their eggs or chicks. Yet there can be more to inter-species relationships than meets the eye. Toco toucans have a particular taste for hyacinth macaw eggs, accounting for more than half of losses. Yet tocos are also fond of the fruits of the *manduvi* tree (*Sterculia apetala*) and are responsible for more than four-fifths of seed dispersal. More than 90% of hyacinth macaw pairs nest in *manduvi*. Since the macaw population – as a whole and over time – depends on replenishment of the *manduvi* stock, it is best served by a large (if egg-thieving) toucan population. Some individual macaws take a hit – but for the greater good of their species. Conservationists are now factoring in such conflicting ecological pressures to their management decisions. Nature is never simple.

WOODPECKERS

Anyone who thinks the Pantanal is just about wetlands should pause to contemplate its woodpeckers (Picidae). No other bird family is so inextricably linked with trees – so the fact that visitors can see ten species in an average Pantanal trip suggests that the region must have plenty of woodland. Woodpeckers have evolved to cling to vertical trunks, with stiffened tail feathers offering support and strong feet – two toes pointing forwards and two backwards – to grip the trunk. Robust bills enable them to hammer into branches so that their long barb-tipped tongue can reach far into a cavity to extract insect larvae.

Lineated woodpecker. (OP)

Pantanal woodpeckers vary in weight from just 10g to nearly 200g. At the bottom end of the scale are piculets, miniature woodpeckers that creep along the slimmest of branches on the shortest of trees. White-barred piculets (*Picumnus cirratus*) inhabit forests whereas white-wedged piculets (*P. albosquammatus*) reside in open country. Campo flickers (*Colaptes campestris*) are also open-country specialists – largely terrestrial woodpeckers that feast on ants and termites. They are gregarious – as are the white woodpecker (*Melanerpes candidus*) and, in the far south, white-fronted woodpecker (*M. cactorum*). Closely related, these noisy, striking and active birds inhabit forested savannas.

In forest, there are woodpeckers at all levels. The little woodpecker (*Veniliornis passerinus*) and checkered woodpecker (*V. mixtus*) forage mainly low down. In the mid-storey, look for two larger, verdent brethren: golden-green woodpecker (*Piculus chrysochloros*) and green-barred woodpecker (*Colaptes melanochloros*). The trio of *Celeus* woodpeckers are yellow and black with a long, erectile crest. This coiffure reaches punk proportions in the blond-crested woodpecker (*C. flavescens*), leading to the birders' nickname of 'Billy Idol' woodpecker, in homage to the shock-locked 1980s rocker. More widespread is the pale-crested woodpecker (*C. lugubris*), while the cream-coloured woodpecker (*C. flavus*) takes the genus's yellow pigmentation to the extreme, retaining just dark wings and tail. The largest woodpeckers are typically found at the top of the tallest trees. All are black-and-white with a mainly red head. To differentiate them, pay particular attention to the pale markings: the cream-backed woodpecker (*Campephilus leucopogon*) has an ivory mantle, while the crimson-crested (*C. melanoleucus*) has a whiter face than the lineated (*Dryocopus lineatus*).

Campo flickers are open-country birds. (JL)

The quintessential ovenbird, this rufous hornero sits atop its dome-shaped mud nest. (JL)

PASSERINES

Half the world's birds are classified as passerines. This order is characterised by having three forward-facing toes and one backward-pointing toe that meet the foot at the same level. This morphological adaptation enables passerines (or 'perching birds') to grasp a branch, toes locking into position even when the bird is asleep. All songbirds are passerines – although not all passerines are songbirds.

OVENBIRDS

Ovenbirds or furnariids are a large, diverse family of insectivores whose dull plumage shrouds lives that are far from boring. Ovenbirds have radiated into almost every South American habitat, occupying finely separated ecological niches. The Pantanal's 15 or so species variously inhabit open scrub, thickets, riverbanks, cerrado, marshes and dense forest. The family name derives from the horneros (*Furnarius*), which build dome-shaped mud nests that resemble a traditional baker's oven (*horno* in Spanish).

Striding jauntily along the ground or duetting loudly from a tree with its partner, a rufous hornero (*Furnarius rufus*) – the best-known furnariid – demands attention. Its nest-building process is a labour of love, a pair needing three weeks to collect sufficient wet mud and straw to construct their two-chambered home. On shady riverbanks, look for a scarcer relative – the pale-legged hornero (*F. leucopus*) – strutting along, distinguished by a white stripe behind the eye.

Spinetails are predominantly arboreal ovenbirds with weedy bills and long tails. Members of the genus *Synallaxis* skulk in dense vegetation; obtusely, this obfuscatory habit endears these birds to birders, who are keen to see Pantanal specialities such as white-lored (*S. albilora*) and cinereous-breasted spinetails (*S. hypospodia*). A similar bird with an absurdly long tail will be a chotoy spinetail (*Schoeniophylax phryhanophilus*). During the breeding season, this yellow-chinned denizen of scrub and cerrado marks its presence with a large, spherical stick-nest. Prominent nests also alert birders to rufous-fronted thornbirds (*Phacellodomus rufifrons*), which weave a heap of sticks around a vertical branch, and to firewood-gatherers (*Anumbius annumbi*) and rufous cacholotes (*Pseudoseisura unirufa*), which both build large stick nests in a tree fork.

The rufous cacholote is one of the more striking furnariids, with its bright plumage and staring eye. (JL)

Like all its kind, the narrow-billed woodcreeper only ever climbs up trees, never down them. (JL)

WOODCREEPERS

You might surmise that a large, brown, strong-billed bird spiralling up a tree would be a woodpecker. Not so. The bird is one of ten species of woodcreeper (Dendrocolaptidae), an unrelated family whose arboreal habits have converged with those of woodpeckers. The most common species is the narrow-billed woodcreeper (*Lepidocolaptes angustirostris*), which has a bold eyestripe and downcurved bill. The most impressive family members are great rufous woodcreeper (*Xiphocolaptes major*) and red-billed scythebill (*Campylorhamphus trochilirostris*). The former is a sturdy-billed giant, easily as big as the largest Pantanal woodcreeper, usually adorning isolated trees in open terrain. As its name suggests, the scythebill has a remarkable bill that is very long, sharply downcurved and bright crimson.

ANTBIRDS

The male barred antshrike is well named. (JL)

So named for their association with – rather than consumption of – ants, antbirds (Thamnophilidae) are a diverse collection of stocky passerines, some of which follow army ant (*Eciton*) swarms to feast on invertebrates forced to flee by the marching column. In order of increasing size, the Pantanal's 15 members comprise antvireos, antwrens, antbirds and antshrikes. The most attractive antwrens are the large-billed (*Herpsilochmus longirostris*) and the rusty-backed (*Formicivora rufa*). The former inhabits gallery forest, and the startlingly cinnamon-coloured female is more eye-catching than the monochrome male. The reverse is true of the rusty-backed antwren: the striking male is rufous, black and white, but the female dowdy.

For birders, the most interesting antbirds are the band-tailed (*Hypocnemoides maculicauda*) and the Mato Grosso (*Cercomacra melanaria*). Both inhabit forest near water and typically forage in pairs. The latter is almost endemic to the Pantanal, and the region marks the southern limit of the range of the former, an Amazonian species. Antshrikes are the easiest members of the family to see, particularly the great antshrike (*Taraba major*) and the barred antshrike (*Thamnophilus doliatus*). In both cases, unless you saw a pair together, it would be easy to conclude that males and females belong to separate species. Only a flaming red eye connects the black-and-white male great antshrike to the rufous female. The female barred antshrike, unmarked and gingery, lacks the male's monochrome barring that gives the species its English name. For those interested in taxonomy, the most fascinating species is the planalto slaty-antshrike (*T. pelzelni*). This is one of seven species recently 'split' – on the basis of DNA and vocalisations – from what was formerly considered a single species, eastern slaty-antshrike (*T. punctuatus*).

TYRANT-FLYCATCHERS

The most speciose family in the New World, with 380 members, tyrant-flycatchers (Tyrannidae) are also one of the most heterogeneous. The most widespread and familiar of the Pantanal's 60 species, the great kiskadee (*Pitangus sulphuratus*) is ten times heavier than the smallest, the common tody-flycatcher (*Todriostrum cinereum*). Most tyrannids have short tails, but the fork-tailed flycatcher (*Tyrannus savanna*) and streamer-tailed tyrant (*Gubernetes yetapa*) have dramatically long, forked appendages. Most tyrants are dowdy birds, clad in greys and greens, but several splash out on a flash of colour with a semi-concealed yellow or orange crown-stripe; two – the vermilion flycatcher (*Pyrocephalus rubinus*) and the cliff flycatcher (*Hirundinea ferruginea*) – break rank completely, being largely pink and terracotta respectively. But such variation is countered by incredible similarity between members of individual genera: even experienced ornithologists have problems distinguishing between species in the genera *Elaenia* (dull olive birds with white wingbars), *Myiozetetes* (like miniature kiskadees) and *Myiarchus* (brown flycatchers with yellow bellies).

The great kiskadee is a familiar sight around Pantanal lodges. (JL)

Elaenia is one of several genera whose members sing exclusively at dawn, a habit so well known in Brazil that it has led to the colloquial name *Maria-já-é-dia* ('Maria, it's daytime!'). Smaller and longer-tailed are the various tyrannulet genera, the most common species being the southern beardless-tyrannulet (*Camptostoma obsoletum*). In isolated areas of cerrado, birders search for the cock-tailed tyrant (*Alectrurus tricolor*), a bizarre and rare flycatcher that communicates via an impressive display flight instead of song. Others, such as the white-throated kingbird (*Tyrannus albogularis*), do both.

Should such courtship displays reap the desired prize of a mate, tyrant-flycatchers set about nest-building. Most Pantanal species construct simple cup-shaped or spherical nests, although a handful, such as the yellow-olive flycatcher (*Tolmomyias sulphurescens*), create a bag-shaped hanging nest. These structures attract the attention of piratic flycatchers (*Legatus leucophaius*). Uniquely among tyrannids, this stripy-headed insectivore bullies nest-owners into deserting, then steals the nest.

Tyrant-flycatchers occur in every habitat. In open country, look for the white monjita (*Xolmis irupero*) and grey monjita (*X. cinereus*), the vermilion flycatcher and the cattle tyrant (*Machetornis rixosa*). The last of these often hitches a ride on livestock or capybara (*Hydrochaeris hydrochaeris*),

Wires offer the vermillion flycatcher convenient perches from which to hawk their insect prey. (JL)

Cattle tyrants often use mammals, here a female marsh deer, as a base from which to hunt insects. (JL)

flitting to the ground to grab insects that the mammals disturb. In scrub, look for several small species with 'tody' in their name, particularly the rusty-fronted tody-flycatcher (*Poecilotriccus latirostris*) and stripe-necked tody-tyrant (*Hemitriccus striaticollis*). The black-backed water-tyrant (*Fluvicola albiventer*) and white-headed marsh-tyrant (*Arundinicola leucocephala*) specialise in foraging in wetlands. In forests, bran-coloured flycatchers (*Myiophobus fasciatus*) sally for arthropods while blending into low vegetation, while the bizarre southern antpipit (*Corythopis delalandi*) pursues insects along the ground.

ON THE BRINK

In life, we have neither the money nor the time to do everything we would like. Prioritisation is essential for every business and every organisation. And so it is for conservationists, self-appointed guardians of nature with the collective goal of preventing extinctions. Published by the World Conservation Union, the IUCN Red List of Threatened Species provides the global

The world population of chestnut-bellied guan may be as low as 1,000 birds, many around the Transpantaneira highway. (JL)

prioritisation, identifying species most in need of conservation attention if global extinction rates are to be reduced. The Red List has further in-built prioritisation. 'Vulnerable' species have a 10% chance of extinction within 100 years; for 'Critically Endangered', the equivalent figures are 50% and 10 years. Species that almost qualify are listed as 'Near Threatened' and those too poorly known to be assessed are 'Data Deficient'. BirdLife International manages the classification of the world's birds, more than 1,200 of which are globally threatened. The Pantanal hosts at least nine – among them the near-endemic chestnut-bellied guan – plus ten Near Threatened species. Protecting the Pantanal helps save these birds from extinction.

The fiery-plumaged band-tailed manakin. (OP)

MANAKINS

In the gloom of the forest, two fireballs tremble and shake before zipping upwards with a mechanical buzz. These rival male band-tailed manakins (*Pipra fasciicauda*) are displaying at a traditional 'lek' site, each seeking to demonstrate its fitness to females. Males of this breathtaking species are bright red on the head, 'fading' to vivid yellow on the vent. Impressive displays are almost universal among manakins (Pipridae). Helmeted manakins (*Antilophia galeata*) do not lek, but make looping flights between canopy trees. Males are jet-black save for a flaming mantle stripe that culminates in a forward-pointing crest.

But elaborate plumage is not a prerequisite for enticing displays. The localised pale-bellied tyrant-manakin (*Neopelma pallescens*) may not be much to look at but – should there be any chance of mating – it certainly performs, jumping vertically, beating its wings and calling loudly.

VIREOS AND ALLIES

The four members of the Vireonidae are spread across three genera that inhabit the forest edge. The Pantanal's resident red-eyed vireo (*Vireo olivaceus*) population is swelled in summer by migrants from North America. Some ornithologists consider the two to be separate species, given their differences in wing structure and iris colour. Rufous-browed peppershrikes (*Cyclarhis gujanensis*) are robust passerines with a notably hook-tipped bill designed to chop up caterpillars. Similar in plumage, but slender and slim-billed is the ashy-headed greenlet (*Hylophilus pectoralis*), which picks its way delicately through foliage.

JAYS

Jays are the only Neotropical crows (Corvidae). The three Pantanal species – large, charismatic birds with a sharp bill – belong in the same genus (*Cyanocorax*). In plumage and character, however, they have little in common. The purplish jay (*C. cyanomelas*) sits demurely, its ashy-lilac plumage merging with shadows. The brash, raucous plush-crested jay (*C. chrysops*) could not be more different, possessing startling electric-blue face patches and velvety head ruff. Between them lies the curl-crested jay (*C. cristatellus*), less extravagant in plumage but with a teddy boy-like quiff; this cerrado specialist is patchily distributed in the Pantanal.

Purplish jays sometimes sit demurely around lodge buildings. (JL)

SWALLOWS AND MARTINS

Whether lining up on wires prior to migration or gracefully capturing aerial insects, swallows and martins (Hirundinidae) are universally enjoyed. Fittingly, swallows are symbols of peace and happiness in Brazil. There are nine species in the Pantanal, of which visitors should see four or more. Along rivers, look for the southern rough-winged swallows (*Stelgidopteryx ruficollis*): the common name derives from the roughened edge of the male's outermost flight feather, the purpose of which remains a mystery. Over wetlands, white-rumped (*Tachycineta leucorrhoa*) and

White-winged swallows are a common sight around watercourses. (HP)

white-winged swallows (*T. albiventer*) vie for the observer's attention. Given that both have white rumps, you should concentrate on the wings to distinguish one from the other. Around human habitation, large hirundines that recall falcons are brown-chested martins (*Progne tapera*), one of few family members with a dawn song.

WRENS AND ALLIES

With its sweet, melodious warble, the perky house wren (*Troglodytes aedon*) is one of South America's most-loved birds. The antics of this restless little brown job captivate visitors

around lodge buildings. Another wren (Troglodytidae) often found around lodge gardens – if they have palms, on which this species depends – is the thrush-like wren (*Campylorhynchus turdinus*). The comparison with a thrush (*Turdus*) enshrined in the wren's name is due to the latter's size, long bill and lengthy tail. Hardened birders may wish to seek out three *Thrythorus* wrens that differ more in voice than plumage: the moustached (*T. genibarbis*), buff-breasted (*T. leucotis*) and fawn-breasted (*T. guarayanus*). Pair members duet in perfect synchrony; each pair also develops its own particular phraseology or pace to differentiate itself from neighbours.

Another bird that bonds through voice is the black-capped donacobius (*Donacobius atricapilla*). Pairs' vocal explosions are a characteristic sound of Pantanal swamps. Baffled scientists used to treat the donacobius as a wren, but now allocate it to its own family (Donacobiidae). Another group of uncertain evolutionary provenance is the gnatcatchers and gnatwrens, previously classified as Old World warblers (Sylviidae) but now graciously accorded their own family (Polioptilidae).

The diminutive masked gnatcatcher forages daintily for insects in trees. (JL)

Gnatcatchers are dainty arboreal insectivores with slender physiques and long tails. Masked gnatcatchers (*Polioptila dumicola*) usually forage in pairs, the male's head enveloped in a black bandit mask.

THRUSHES, MOCKINGBIRDS AND PIPITS

One of Brazil's oft-cited literary quotations immortalises a thrush: 'My land has palms, where the thrush sings,' wrote Antônio Gonçalves Dias. The irony is that the 19th-century poet was thinking of a mockingbird (Mimidae) – but this in itself suggests a degree of similarity that is reflected in their stocky, long-tailed appearance and vocal mastery. Of the Pantanal's four thrushes (Turdidae), two are relatively common. A garden bird over much

Rufous-bellied thrushes inhabit mainly forest in the Pantanal. (JL)

of South America, the rufous-bellied thrush (*Turdus rufiventris*) is primarily a forest species here, as is the pale-breasted thrush (*T. leucomelas*). In the austral winter (May–August), warmth-loving creamy-bellied thrushes (*T. amaurochalinus*) migrate north to the Pantanal, swelling the thrush ranks.

Mockingbirds exhibit a similar pattern: white-banded mockingbirds (*Mimus triurus*) are a scarce winter visitor, joining the resident chalk-browed mockingbirds (*M. saturninus*). More slender and longer-necked than thrushes, these accomplished mimics jog along the ground as they forage for insects and seeds. A smaller streaked bird sprinting through long grass is usually a yellowish pipit (*Anthus lutescens*), the Pantanal's only representative of the Motacillidae (which, in the Old World, also contains wagtails). This species sings exclusively in flight – a surprisingly rare habit among birds.

TANAGERS, CARDINALS AND ALLIES

Male swallow tanager. (JL)

Tanagers (Thraupidae) are often a kaleidoscope of colour. In lodge gardens, look for palm tanagers (*Thraupis palmarum*) hogging palms as songposts, while closely related sayaca tanagers (*T. sayaca*) guzzle fruit nearby. In forests, common thraupids include the grey-headed tanager (*Eucometis penicillata*) and silver-beaked tanager (*Ramphocelus carbo*), both stocky birds with powerful bills. Silver-beaked tanagers would be hard to spot were it not for their swollen lower mandible gleaming in the gloom. In the tallest trees, look for the bizarre swallow tanager (*Tersina viridis*); the male is electric blue, the female bright green. Unlike most thraupids, this nomadic species hawks for insects in small family groups. Another oddity is a tiny bird with plumage recalling that of a greater kiskadee but sipping nectar from forest flowers – a bananaquit (*Coereba flaveola*). This bird baffles

The red-crested cardinal tends to occur singly or in pairs, often near watercourses. (JL)

Double-collared seedeater. (JL)

ornithologists, who can never agree on its taxonomic affinities: is it related to tanagers, grassquits (*Tiaris*) or wood-warblers (Parulidae)?

If you find yourself in cerrado, look for two striking and rare thraupids: the white-banded (*Neothraupis fasciata*) and white-rumped (*Cypsnagra hirundinacea*) tanagers. Both are largely black and white, although the former has grey upperparts and the latter a cinnamon throat. Given their wider habitat preferences and greater abundance, you are more likely to come across boisterous, crimson-headed cardinals. The red-crested cardinal (*Paroaria coronata*) is unmistakable with its long, erect crest; it is usually near water. The gregarious yellow-billed cardinal (*P. capitata*) hangs out in large flocks around stables (see page 154), a habit that leads to its Brazilian name of *cavalaria* (cavalry).

SPARROWS, SEEDEATERS AND FINCHES

Around 25 members of the sparrow family (Emberizidae) occur in the Pantanal, mostly in grassland. Flocks of yellow-finches (*Sicalis*) are a common sight, but species are hard to distinguish from one another: the most common are the saffron finch (*S. flaveola*) and grassland yellow-finch (*S. luteola*). Beware that only the males are yellow; the females are brown and heavily streaked. Apparently equally nondescript is the grassland sparrow (*Ammodramus humeralis*) which runs along the ground like a mouse.

However, this subtle songster rewards close scrutiny, displaying chestnut in the wing and a yellow spot before the eye.

Seedeaters comprise nearly half the family, although ornithologists are still determining where one species stops and another starts. Males and females differ markedly in plumage: males are clad in black, white, blue or rufous, whereas females are plain brown. Double-collared (*Sporophila caerulescens*), rusty-collared (*S. collaris*) and white-bellied seedeaters (*S. leucoptera*) often flock together to feed on grass seeds, bending a stem to the ground so as to feed in comfort.

Two smart emberizids break their family's open-country mould, inhabiting scrub and woodland. The scarlet plumage of the red-crested finch (*Coryphospingus cucullatus*) contrasts with its demure demeanour. The saffron-billed sparrow (*Arremon flavirostris*) is similarly striking yet reclusive, its plumage a medley of black, white, grey and green. The true finches (Fringillidae) are mainly Old World birds, but the New World also has a few representatives. In a Pantanal context, these comprise a trio of euphonias (*Euphonia*), dumpy frugivores with stubby bills.

A singing saffron-billed sparrow. (JL)

A male saffron finch. (JL)

WOOD-WARBLERS

A flash of yellow in the undergrowth catches the eye. It is most likely a tropical parula (*Parula pitiayumi*) or flavescent warbler (*Basileuterus flaveolus*) – both vividly coloured residents of Pantanal forests. Wood-warblers (Parulidae) are small, slim insectivores that hover or glean their prey from under leaves. They are restless birds, forever on the move, but often curious towards human observers. A close approach from a tropical parula is likely to be a memorable experience, as this gem has blue upperparts, bright yellow underparts and an orange wash to the breast. Masked yellowthroats (*Geothlypis aequinoctialis*) differ from other Pantanal warblers in having separate male and female plumages (only the male has a black eye-mask), and inhabiting damp scrub rather than forest.

A male masked yellowthroat. (JL)

Orange-backed troupials are regular visitors to lodge gardens. (OP)

BLACKBIRDS

The combined life stories of blackbirds (Icteridae) would make for a fantastic soap opera. All necessary elements are present: beauty, infidelity, deception and theft – and all conducted at top volume. Icterids comprise four distinct groups, each with specific roles in the show: oropendulas and caciques; orioles; blackbirds; and cowbirds.

Crested oropendulas (*Psarocolius decumanus*) and caciques, such as the yellow-rumped (*Cacicus cela*) and golden-winged (*C. chrysopterus*), have a swollen bill base that, in the oropendula, projects well up the forehead. The two genera have similar nests – hanging baskets of moss up to 2m long. With one exception – the well-named solitary black cacique (*C. solitarius*) – caciques are noisy colonial breeders. There are few more quintessentially Neotropical sights than a bevy of oropendula nests swinging from a tall palm.

The nuts of *buriti* palms are among the favoured foods of the orange-backed troupial (*Icterus croconotus*), a slender oriole attired in a heart-stopping combination of orange and black. The troupial shares with the promiscuous bay-winged cowbird (*Agelaioides badius*) a disreputable tendency to take over other species' nests and use them as its own. This piratical behaviour is eclipsed by that of other cowbirds, which are true brood parasites. They lay eggs in other species' nests and play no further role in the parental process. Shiny cowbirds (*Molothrus bonariensis*) are known to parasitise 60 species.

The other two cowbirds are more selective, focusing their attentions, ironically, on fellow icterids: screaming cowbirds (*M. rufoaxillarius*) target bay-winged cowbirds; giant cowbirds (*M. oryzivorus*) focus on caciques and oropendulas.

The five species of blackbird are less scandalous in behaviour. Three are associated with wetlands and two with grasslands. One wetland species, the scarlet-headed blackbird (*Amblyramphus holosericeus*), is an expert at 'gaping', an extraordinary foraging behaviour unique to icterids. The bird inserts its pointed bill into a fruit then opens its mandibles to get at any food hidden within.

Shiny cowbirds may be associated with cattle, but also frequent horses. (JL)

Reptiles, Amphibians and Fish

REPTILES

No class of animals evokes more trepidation than reptiles (Reptilia). Even that most heinous of human crimes, murder 'in cold blood', invokes these ectothermic creatures, which are guilty of no more than an inability to generate their own body heat. Our fear has been enshrined in reptilian beasts of lore: dragons appear from the era of St George to that of Shrek, and basilisks slither from Greek mythology to Harry Potter's chamber of secrets. But few real reptiles are remotely as dangerous as their legendary counterparts, and the Pantanal is a fantastic place for herpetophobes to move from worry to wonder, with around 80 species to marvel at.

Traditional taxonomy recognises three orders of reptile in South America: Chelonia (tortoises and turtles), Crocodylia (crocodilians) and Squamata (lizards, amphisbaenians and snakes). The application of molecular biology, however, suggests a radically different treatment may be more appropriate (see page 92, *Is a caiman a bird?*). For now we follow the conventional approach, which unites animals that are covered with scaly skin and breathe through lungs rather than gills. As reptiles are cold-blooded, their lives revolve around regulating temperature, moving between sun and shade (or water) as required, and – in the case of crocodilians – opening their jaws to offload excess heat.

TORTOISES AND TURTLES

The order Chelonia is characterised by ostentatious in-house security. Hard shells cover all but head and limbs – and even these can be safely retracted under the carapace. With this almost impregnable fortress, unchanged for 200 million years, survival rates are high and lifespans long for chelonids that make it to adulthood. Tortoises (family Testudinidae) have a domed shell and live on land. Turtles (Chelidae), with their flatter shell and slender limbs, are streamlined for a largely aquatic life.

Red-footed tortoise is the more common of the Pantanal's two tortoises. (JCS/FLPA)

Of the 300-odd members of this order worldwide, the Pantanal has a miserly four: two from each family. The tortoises are herbivores that use strong jawbones to chomp through terrestrial vegetation. When a red-footed tortoise (*Chelonoides carbonaria*) feels infested with ectoparasites, it heads for an ant nest and allows the inhabitants to forage over its skin. The other tortoise is so rare that herpetologists can't agree on an English name. But whatever you call it – the Argentine, Chaco or southern wood tortoise (*C. petersi*) – this species is

Pantanal swamp turtle (FFAC)

particularly threatened by capture for the pet trade. Distinguishing the two species is easy: the red-footed tortoise has red spots on its forelimbs and a more ridged shell.

As its name suggests, the Pantanal swamp turtle (*Acanthochelys macrocephala*) is a speciality of the world's largest wetland. This is a 'side-necked turtle', so-called because it retracts the neck sideways when withdrawing into its shell. It eluded discovery until as recently as 1984, perhaps because it slumbers through the dry season in soft mud, emerging only with subsequent rains. This turtle is scarce, with conservationists considering it at potential future risk of extinction. The same applies to Vanderhaege's toad-headed turtle (*Mesoclemmys vanderhaegei*), a carnivorous chelid famed for its aggressiveness.

CAIMAN

Crocodilians are among the most ancient of living reptiles, their form having scarcely changed in 100 million years. With a muscular tail, hefty jaws, superlative strength and razor-sharp teeth, these are the bruisers of the reptile school. Little wonder that the immense seasonal gatherings of their Pantanal representative – the yacaré caiman, or simply yacaré (*Caiman yacare*) – are one of the biggest wildlife attractions in South America.

There are six species of *Caiman*, all restricted to the Neotropics and all in the

A yacaré's teeth are the ultimate fish trap. (AL)

family Alligatoridae. The yacaré has only recently been declared a species in its own right, having formerly been lumped with the spectacled caiman (*C. crocodilus*), which occurs farther north. These animals, like all crocodilians, are adapted for hunting by stealth. Their eyes and nostrils lie above the line of the body, enabling them to see and breathe while otherwise concealed by water or vegetation. Such features enable predator to approach victim without being detected. Should a caiman submerge for the final attack,

Yacaré gather during the dry season in large groups around remaining waterbodies. (RT)

it lowers flaps over its throat, nostrils and ears to prevent water entering, and protects its eyes with transparent eyelids.

Although the yacaré is one of the world's smaller crocodilians, it nevertheless reaches lengths of 2–3m. In the Pantanal, typical prey comprises capybara, herons and fish. In the dry season, yacaré make a beeline for remaining ponds. Hundreds congregate *en masse*, lying parallel in the shallows and turning floating water hyacinths (*Eichhornia crassipes*) into a morass of scaly armour. The purpose of these gatherings is twofold: to avoid drying out and to indulge in the drought's fishy feast. This gives photographers the opportunity for that quintessential Pantanal image – a cluster of caiman waiting for fish to flop into their jaws against a blurred backdrop of flowing water. For a fresher experience, head into the night with a torch and enjoy the reflections of hundreds of crocodilian eyes, gleaming like lacustrine stars. Then listen to the caimans roar, lifting their heads clear of the water so that the sound carries farther.

Seeing such hordes, you might think that yacaré are abundant. And you would be right – but only because of recent conservation efforts. For almost the entire 20th century, Pantanal caiman suffered catastrophic levels of hunting to supply the global demand for crocodile shoes. Even during the 1980s, a million yacaré were harvested annually. Only since 1990 has new trade legislation been sufficiently enforced for poaching to cease. Yacaré have recovered rapidly, and the current population may be around 35 million, with densities ten times higher than the 1970s. Nowadays, the yacaré is one reptile that you will see on even the briefest Pantanal visit.

IS A CAIMAN A BIRD?

Based on fossil evidence, evolutionary biologists have long surmised that reptiles, dinosaurs and birds were closely related. But recent evidence from molecular and genetic studies has blown from the water our traditional understanding of what constitutes a 'reptile'. The most sensational finding is that crocodiles – including the Pantanal's yacaré caiman – appear to be more closely related to birds than they are to other reptiles such as lizards. If true, this would require a major overhaul of our animal classification system – enough to make any scientist's mind boggle. For now, it seems simpler to stick with our conventional understanding of reptiles.

Green (or common) iguanas are often spied basking, and scratching, beside water. (JL)

LIZARDS

Lizards are the four-legged members of the order Squamata – allowing for a few that have only two legs or even none at all. The score of Pantanal species vary in size from geckos just 5cm long to iguanas that exceed 2m. Many lizards have a nifty, if rather dramatic, way of escaping danger. If a predator seizes their tail, they snap it off at a predetermined weak point. This leaves the predator with a wriggling tail tip – a decent, fatty meal in itself – while the lizard makes a getaway, regrowing its tail over time.

Iguana

The dragon of fables has its roots in a very real group of reptiles: the iguanas (Iguanidae). The Pantanal representative is the green or common iguana (*Iguana iguana*), a standard item in pet shops. With a spiny crest running the length of its back, this lizard has a fearsome appearance but is actually a placid vegetarian. Its beautiful lime-grey coloration provides excellent camouflage as it sprawls along a leafy branch above a river. Get too close to a resting animal, however, and it may plop into the water and swim to tranquillity.

Anoles and spiny lizards

Close relatives of iguanas, though much smaller, are anoles (Polychrotidae) and spiny lizards (Tropuridae). Shared features include the fleshy throat fan that males erect in display. The Pantanal's only anole is the point-nosed false chameleon (*Polychrus acutirostris*), whose eyes have a scaly appearance like those of a true chameleon. Spiny lizards (*Tropidurus* sp.) frequent dry areas such as grasslands, in contrast to brown leaf lizards (*Stenocercus caducus*), which blend in with the litter layer in humid forests.

Tegus are the Americas' equivalent of Old World monitor lizards; this is a black tegu. (OP)

Teiid lizards

A crashing in shrubbery is not always a mammal; tegus (family Teiidae) reach 1m in length and make a racket as they flee from danger on powerful legs. These are the New World equivalent of Old World monitors (*Varanus* sp.), with similar long claws for digging and forked tongue flicked out to 'taste' the air. The common or gold tegu (*Tupinambis teguixin*) occurs in gallery forests and the black tegu (*T. merianae*) in drier habitats. Other members of this complex genus may occur, including one species possibly new to science. The caiman lizard (*Dracaena paraguayensis*) is tegu-sized; its genus name comes from the Greek *drakaina* (female dragon), while the English name is a reference to its spiny, crocodilian protrusions along back and tail. Whereas caiman lizard and tegu exude power, smaller teiids such as the green junglerunner or giant racerunner (*Ameiva ameiva*) embody speed – in name and nature. When not sprinting, the racerunner basks in sunny spots, its white flank spots and stripes gleaming.

Geckos, skinks and microteiids

The Pantanal's remaining lizards fall into three families: geckos (Gekkonidae), skinks (Scincidae) and microteiids or spectacled lizards (Gymophthalmidae). Geckos have modified toe tips that enable them to scale even smooth vertical surfaces. Native to Asia, house geckos

The house gecko is a species native to Asia that has been inadvertently introduced to South America. (MW/FLP)

(*Hemidactylus mabouia*) are invasive aliens, and their arrival may be adversely affecting two native geckos: Wetzel's (*Lygodactylus wetzeli*) and Chacoan leaf-footed (*Phyllopezus pollicaris*). Skinks are slender, smooth-skinned and small-eyed lizards that appear neckless. Uniquely among reptiles, some female skinks nourish their embryos via a placenta. The three Pantanal species belong to the genus *Mabuya*; look for black-spotted skink (*M. nigropunctata*) sunning itself on the forest edge. The microteiids comprise more than 25 genera, but only two species occur in the Pantanal. Schreiber's spectacled lizard (*Cercosaura schreibersii*) can see with its eye closed, thanks to a transparent lower eyelid.

AMPHISBAENIANS

Few Pantanal animals are as unearthly in appearance as amphisbaenians or worm lizards – legless cylinders with concentric rings of scales that move in concertina fashion. Four species occur, including the white amphisbaenid (*Amphisbaena alba*). The group's fondness for lodging in ant nests, with their labyrinth of tunnels and ready supply of food, confused indigenous Brazilians, who named them 'ant kings'. Amphisbaenids' subterranean existence means that they are seen only when heavy rain forces them to surface.

The yellow anaconda is one of the world's biggest snakes. (BL)

SNAKES

Snakes bear most blame for reptiles' poor public image. From the Garden of Eden onwards, snakes have been identified with evil, evoking fear and loathing in equal measure. Many would-be wildlife-watchers cite snakes as their reason for avoiding the tropics. Yet many societies worship snakes as symbols of health and rejuvenation. And the grounds for distress are slight: less than 10% of snakes are venomous, and even fewer pose any threat to humans. Moreover, seeing any snake is a challenge; most are secretive, nocturnal and far more scared of you than you are of them. The Pantanal hosts around 50 species spread across at least five families. Ditch the dread and revel in a suite of animals as beautiful and diverse as any!

A sizeable yellow anaconda, watched by two rather nervous whistling herons. (EW)

Snakes have much in common. With poor eyesight and hearing, almost all rely on their flickering tongue to gather olfactory information. All, moreover, are carnivores that swallow their prey whole. But there are differences that relate to ecological niches. A snake's shape fits its domain. Burrowing snakes are short and stout, arboreal serpents long and lithe. Snakes also move in different ways; not all slither. Those with thick bodies pull themselves forward in linear fashion. Small or arboreal snakes wriggle from side to side. And burrowing snakes move like a concertina through solid earth.

The beautiful patterning of the Brazilian redtail boa assists camouflage. (CdJ)

Blind snakes

Evolutionary biologists believe that snakes evolved from a group of limbless, burrowing reptiles. One group of serpents never even made it above ground: the blind snakes (superfamily Scolecophida), represented in the Pantanal by the black blind snake (*Typhlops brongersmianus*). Your best chance of seeing this sightless creature is after heavy rain, when its subterranean tunnels are flooded.

Anacondas and boas

One serpent both tops most visitors' Pantanal 'wish list' and scoops first prize for the world's biggest snake: the anaconda. There are two species in the region: the yellow anaconda (*Eunectes notaeus*) and the green anaconda (*E. murinus*). The latter is the larger (reaching 6m and 250kg), but also the rarer, being at the southern end of its range. Yellow anacondas rarely reach more than 4m, but even that makes for a spectacle. Both species are adapted for aquatic life in or around shallow water. Like caiman, they have elevated eyes and nostrils that allow them to see and breathe while otherwise submerged. This enables them to stalk mammals as large as capybara, which they kill by asphyxiation, constricting the victim within their muscular coils. A good place to look is under bridges, where anacondas often slumber peacefully.

Two other boas, the Brazilian redtail boa or boa constrictor (*Boa constrictor*) and rainbow boa (*Epicrates cenchria*), also squeeze the life out of their prey. Both are beautifully patterned, although the markings aim to provide camouflage rather than appeal to aesthetic sensibility. Largely arboreal, boas wait motionless in trees, using pits running along the upper jaw to detect changes in heat distribution that indicate an approaching mammal. With such advanced perceptiveness, who needs sharp eyesight?

Vipers

Vipers (Viperidae) also use heat-sensing pits to track prey, but kill them by lunging with long, sharp fangs. Penetrating the victim's skin, the fangs release venom that causes internal haemorrhaging then death. Vipers can be aggressive if they feel threatened, so if you spot one, watch from a safe distance. The Mato Grosso lancehead (*Bothrops mattogrossensis*) is relatively common on warm nights near wetlands. Herpetologists think that its long tail helps it climb into trees during floods. This species is more densely patterned than the Brazilian lancehead (*B. moojeni*), a

The South American rattlesnake rattles its warning only when it feels threatened. (HP)

frequent road-kill victim. South American rattlesnake (*Crotalus durissus*) bites can be very dangerous. However, it is in neither your interest nor the snake's for it to waste venom on a mammal it cannot eat, so if you get too close, a helpful rattling of the hard scales at its tail tip will sound a warning.

The Brazilian lancehead is more active by night than by day. (PO/FLPA)

Coral snakes – real and false

Elapids (Elapidae) eclipse even vipers in the venom stakes. Outside South America, this family includes cobras and mambas. The only Pantanal elapid is the Argentinian coral snake (*Micrurus pyrrhocryptus*). Its black, white and red colouration warns potential predators that it is poisonous. Most predators get the message and stay away. Other snakes have cottoned onto this ruse, mimicking the coral's colour pattern. Pantanal examples include the harmless false coral snake (*Oxyrhopus rhombifer*). But this strategy is not foolproof: a burrowing owl (*Athene cunicularia*) has been recorded killing *Oxyrhopus*, and laughing falcons (*Herpetotheres cachinnans*) readily eat both coral snakes and their mimics.

The colour pattern of the banded calico snake (*Oxyrhopus petola*) signifies that it is a false coral snake. (LVC)

Lichtenstein's green racer is at home on or above ground. (HP)

Colubrids

Most Pantanal serpents, including coral snake mimics, are colubrids (Colubridae). These 'typical snakes' come in many sizes and colours, and live in all manner of habitats. But they have some important similarities. Notably, they have relinquished their left lung to become more slender. A third are venomous, but most of these are back-fanged and thus harmless to humans.

Unsurprisingly in a wetland, several Pantanal colubrids are aquatic. A false water cobra (*Hydrodynastes gigas*) takes its name from the habit of raising a flattened neck prior to striking – like a true cobra (*Naja* sp.). This large reptile packs a vicious bite, so stay clear. If you see a swimming snake with black and orange stripes on its flanks, you are probably watching a leopard

Although largely terrestrial, the regal liophis (*Liophis reginae*) readily ascends small trees. (HP)

kickback (*Helicops leopardinus*), a voracious consumer of Pantanal fish. Among arboreal serpents, tiger ratsnakes (*Spilotes pullatus*) slalom through branches at night, killing roosting birds by constriction. The delicate, jade-coloured parrot snake (*Leptophis ahaetulla*) hunts tree-frogs (Hylidae); when scared, it opens its mouth wide and mock-attacks.

Primarily terrestrial, the indigo snake or yellowtail cribo (*Drymarchon corais*) is an ambush expert that reaches 2m long. Smaller snakes, by contrast, are often speed merchants. These include a handful of liophis or swamp snakes (*Liophis* sp.), and three racers (*Philodryas*). All bar Lichtenstein's green racer (*P. olfersii*) are terrestrial; this species uses the camouflage offered by its vivid green colouration to hunt amidst foliage.

AMPHIBIANS

Amphibians (class Amphibia) were the first vertebrates to set foot on land, having evolved from fish roughly 375 million years ago. Their heyday was their first 100 million years, after which reptiles gradually ousted them from many terrestrial habitats thanks to their ability to lay eggs on land. Many amphibians became extinct – a process that, tragically, is being renewed today (see page 101, *Frog fungus fears*). Amphibians never entirely abandoned their aquatic roots, however. Most depend on water to breed, with juveniles being aquatic (and breathing through gills, like fish) before transmogrifying into adults capable of respiration through their skin. This double life is embodied in the name 'amphibian', from the Greek for 'dual existence'. Two orders of amphibians occur in the Pantanal: frogs and toads – known collectively as anurans (Anura) – and caecilians (Gymnophiona), outlandish creatures that appear part-snake, part-earthworm.

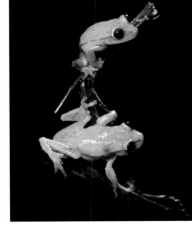

Glass frogs (*Hypsiboas punctata*) are among the Pantanal's 15 tree-frog species. (HP)

The purple-barred tree-frog (*above*) is more than twice the size of the lesser tree-frog (*below*). (Both EvU)

FROGS AND TOADS

Fifty anurans in seven families inhabit the Pantanal, but others may remain to be discovered. All are broad-headed, fat-bodied animals with powerful hind legs that propel them on land and in water. On calm nights, particularly after rain, the Pantanal resounds with the calls of male frogs. Each species-specific vocalisation seeks to attract a female and deter rival males. Listen carefully to the chorus and you may detect a pattern. To avoid being drowned out, individual frogs orchestrate their vocal interventions for the gaps between others' utterances. The result is a beautiful, incessant aural twinkling.

Adult anurans breathe through their skin, an adaptation that unfortunately increases their susceptibility to dehydration. To counter this, they must rest somewhere cool and moist during the day. To tell where that might be, examine a frog's feet: aquatic frogs have prominent webbing between toes to facilitate swimming; arboreal have adhesive pads with which to grip vertical surfaces; and terrestrial frogs have protrusions on their soles to facilitate digging.

Tree-frogs (Hylidae) hog the bottom rung of the anuran size ladder and, in the Pantanal, comprise 15 delicate species in three subfamilies. True tree-frogs (subfamily Hylinae) vary from the 2cm-long dwarf tree-frog (*Dendrosophus nanus*) to the purple-barred tree-frog (*Hypsiboas raniceps*), three times larger. If you hear a frog calling from your bathroom, it will probably be a snouted tree-frog (*Scinax* sp.), which is fond of sinks and showers. Leaf frogs (Phyllomedusinae) have absurdly long legs that serve both to clamber around forest vegetation and to smear lubricant over dehydrating skin – the latter an essential dry season trick. This group contains the remarkable paradox or shrinking frog (*Pseudis paradoxus*), which is unique for having tadpoles three times the size of adults.

Other families are odd in different ways. One-fifth of Pantanal frogs belong to the genus Leptodactylus (*Leptodactylidae*), which, unlike other anurans, pack their eggs in foam nests to protect them from predators. The two horned toads (Ceratophryidae) are

Rococo toads often hunt around lodges. (JL)

aggressive, large-mouthed anurans that think nothing of unprovoked attacks on predators – or each other. When threatened, dwarf frogs (Leiuperidae) such as Natterer's eyed frog (*Eupemphix nattereri*) and weeping dwarf frog (*Physalaemus bilignigerus*) face away from the predator and raise their legs to reveal an eye-like pattern in the groin that gives the impression of a larger animal. Microhylid frogs (Microhylidae) include the yellow-bellied narrow-mouthed frog (*Elachistocleis bicolor*), which has a flattened body, a small pointed head and a taste for termites. Poison frogs (Dendrobatidae) are toxic to any predator silly enough to try eating them. Two species occur, the more widespread being the spot-legged poison frog (*Ameerega picta*), which calls loudly from leaf litter.

Finally, rococo toads (*Rhinella schneideri*; family Bufonidae) love foraging for flies around lodge buildings, where they astound visitors with their size (up to 20cm). If this toad's normal bulk does not deter a would-be predator, it inflates itself beyond the swallowing capabilities of most.

FROG FUNGUS FEARS

In the second half of the 1980s, reports began to emerge of dramatic declines in amphibian populations all over the world. Only recently has the true scale of the crisis become apparent. One-third of the world's amphibian species are now globally threatened or extinct, according to the World Conservation Union. Just 1% has increasing populations. Frogs and their allies are on the brink of disaster. Habitat loss poses the greatest threat, but a newcomer on the block is increasingly perturbing conservationists: fungal disease. First detected in Australia in 1993, herpetologists soon realised that the problem was global. Chytridiomycosis, caused by the chytrid fungus *Batrachochytrium dendrobatidis*, has so far affected 500 frog species, often causing sudden and dramatic population declines that rapidly end in extinction. Although frog deaths due to the fungus have yet to be proven in the Pantanal, this is as likely due to sparse herpetological surveys as actual absence. If (when?) it arrives, there may be no holding back. No control measures are known, so conservationists will be powerless to stop its spread.

CAECILIANS

Caecilians live below ground and are rarely seen. If you dig into moist soil, you may unearth a slimy-skinned legless creature that moves by pushing the front part of its body forward into increasingly taut skin before allowing the hind part to catch up. Once above the soil surface, however, it writhes like a serpent. The ringed caecilian (*Siphonops annulatus*) takes maternal care to a new level. Newborn caecilians feed by exfoliating their mother, eating her outer layer of skin. Three days later, when new skin has grown to replace the old, the young repeat the process – and do so every third day for up to 11 months.

The largespot river stingray swims just above the riverbed. (FWL/FLPA)

FISH

Fish (phylum Chordata) are the only animals in this book whose entire lifecycle is aquatic. They are adapted for underwater existence, with streamlined shapes, friction-reducing scales, fins for power-steering and gills for breathing. Seeing fish is problematic for the land-based wildlife-watcher. You are most likely to spy them in a predator's mouth or beak, splashing frantically in a dessicating pond, wriggling on a fishing line, or – identifiable by taste rather than morphology – laid out at your lunchtime buffet. Nevertheless, fish play an important role in Pantanal ecosystems and are integral to the local culture. An overview of the more prominent species is thus essential for this guide.

Between 270 and 325 species are thought to occur. Almost all are bony fish (class Osteichthyes) – characterised by their strong but light internal skeleton – with just a few cartilaginous fish (class Chondrichthyes). Among bony fish, characins (order Characiformes) and catfish (Siluriformes) each account for 40% of diversity. As with terrestrial animals, species composition depends on habitat. Small characids dominate in rapid rivers, small catfishes on sandy bottoms. Slow, deep waters have the highest diversity – and the most valuable fish for aquarium markets.

CARTILAGINOUS FISH

River stingrays

Cartilaginous fish comprise a trio of river stingrays (Potamotrygonidae). Related to sharks, flat-bodied stingrays swim sinuously just above the river bottom. Resting concealed in the mud, the largespot river stingray (*Potamotrygon falkneri*) defends itself with a sharp spine on the tail: woe betide the shoeless fisherman!

Lungfish

The South American lungfish (*Lepidosiren paradoxa*) is a living fossil that inhabits stagnant waters. The only member of the order Lepidosireniformes, this eel-like creature has a dorsal fin the length of its slender body and a long ventral fin. Whereas most fish succumb to dehydration or predation during the dry season, the lungfish hibernates in mud, leaving holes so that it can breathe.

The South American lungfish sees out the dry season encased in a cocoon of mucus beneath the mud. (AS/SP)

BONY FISH

Characins

A diverse bunch, characins (Characidae) include the Pantanal's most famous fish, the dorado (*Salminus brasiliensis*), and the most notorious, piranhas. If you have heard of only one South American fish, it is surely the piranha, renowned for its numerous, sharp teeth and reputedly voracious appetite. However, it is a myth that piranhas hunt in large packs; sizeable schools actually serve

Spotted piranha (*Serrasalmus marginatus*). (JL)

as defence against predators. Although piranhas occasionally nibble bathing humans, the infamous scene in the James Bond film *You Only Live Twice* bears no relation to reality.

Piranha taxonomy is in a state of flux. Ictythologists disagree on how many genera piranhas comprise – let alone species. A common Pantanal species is the red-bellied piranha (*Pygocentrus nattereri*), which is largely vegetarian. Growing up to 3.5kg and 35cm, it provides bounty for fishermen, with piranha soup being a typical Pantanal dish. A relative, pacu (*Piaractus mesopotamicus*), also often ends up on the menu.

Prized by sport fishers, the dorado or jaw characin is gold-coloured, up to 1m long and 10kg in weight. With powerful jaws replete with sharp teeth, this is a major river predator, consuming birds, small mammals and fish such as sabalo (*Prochilodus lineatus*). Another top predator that captivates sport fishers is the Pantanal pike characin (*Acestrorhynchus pantaneiro*). The slender build and razor-edged teeth of this genus prompt aquarists to name it the 'freshwater barracuda'.

Catfish

Catfish are highly diverse and Pantanal members are spread across ten families. Although morphology varies considerably, many catfish have flattened heads with long snouts and sensory 'whiskers'. These barbels are taken to an extreme in long-whiskered catfish (Pimelodidae), such as spotted surubi or pintado (*Pseudoplatystoma corruscans*) and tiger flathead or surubim (*P. fasciatum*). Having tasty, boneless flesh and regularly measuring up to 90cm (the record is 1.6m and 100kg!), both are targeted by fishermen. In contrast, spiny dwarf catfish (Scoloplacidae) are just 2cm long and were formerly thought to be juveniles of other species. The skin of armoured catfish (Callichthyidae) has overlapping bony plates; the cascarudo (*Callichthys callichthys*) is able to breathe intestinally, which enables it to move overland between water bodies during the dry season.

The dorado is a major river predator that may weigh up to 10kg. (LC/FLPA)

INVERTEBRATES

A swarm of butterflies stocking up on minerals. (CdJ)

The stars of the Pantanal show are undeniably large mammals, striking birds and lithe reptiles. But there would be no spectacle without the backstage staff, a myriad of smaller creatures. The base of the animal food pyramid comprises a vast range of invertebrates that wriggle, bore, buzz and teem through earth, air and water. These spineless critters form 97% of all known animal species and comprise 30 different phyla. There are probably more species in a single phylum – arthropods (Arthropoda) – than in the rest of the animal kingdom combined. It is important to acknowledge the qualifier 'probably', as Pantanal invertebrates are poorly known, even for South America. This is one reason why we limit ourselves to sketching out some of the more visible invertebrate groups and their better-known members.

Male *Diastatops pullata*, abdomen a vibrant scarlet, are a common sight along rivers. (JL)

INSECTS

In evolutionary terms, there is no group of animals more successful than insects. More than one million species have already been identified – and this may be just one-tenth of the final total. Insects owe their success to three main traits. Their small size enables them to occupy tiny niches. They have the potential to breed rapidly and thus make the most of temporary or local food abundance. And, critically, many insects can fly – enabling them both to disperse widely and escape predators.

DRAGONFLIES AND DAMSELFLIES

Of all arthropods, none repay close scrutiny more than dragonflies and damselflies (Odonata). These phenomenal aerial predators exhibit exceptional agility as they execute handbrake turns at up to 30km/h. When perched, they embody gracefulness. Through binoculars, their compound eyes are revealed as an iridescent feat of evolutionary engineering. Damselflies such as the cyan-and-black genus *Acanthagrion* are small and dainty, apparently capable only of weak flights interspersed with long rests. In contrast, dragonflies are robust creatures with powerful, dynamic flight. Unlike the homogeneous damselflies, there are many variations on the dragonfly form. In skimmers (Libellulidae), dashers such as *Micrathyria* have a bulbous base to an otherwise slender abdomen. Amberwings (*Perithemis* sp.) flit repetitively round a small area, their burnt-yellow wings and orange thorax positively glowing. *Diastatops pullata* is common along rivers, the male resplendent with scarlet abdomen and wing bases.

Look for great pondhawk (*Erythemis vesiculosa*) on waterside vegetation. (WP)

CRICKETS AND GRASSHOPPERS, MANTIDS AND ANTLIONS

Crickets and grasshoppers (Orthoptera) are the string section of the insect world, rubbing wings against legs to produce impressively strident sounds for creatures just a few centimetres long. Their combined chirruping creates the Pantanal's background hum. Orthopterans have powerful hind legs, enabling them to leap far from danger. Grasshoppers and locusts are diurnal and herbivorous, and have short antennae, whereas crickets are nocturnal and long-horned – and often carnivorous.

Two distantly related insect orders – mantids (Mantodea) and antlions (Neuroptera) – are patient hunters. The stealthy, camouflaged mantids bide time until a fly ventures within pouncing range. Some praying mantids (family Mantidae) are notorious for the

Up close, a praying mantis takes on an almost extraterrestrial air. (JL)

At the bottom of this conical pit, hidden under the sand, waits a hungry antlion larva. (JL)

An elephant beetle investigates a lodge swimming pool. (KG)

female biting off the male's head during copulation. Amazingly, this cannibalistic act does not impede the male from disseminating his genes. Adult antlions of the family Myrmeleontidae catch insects on the wing and resemble damselflies with club-headed antennae. The larvae, however, are terrestrial ambush-specialists. Excavating a conical sandpit, they lurk at the bottom and wait for an ant to approach the rim – at which point they flick up sand grains to knock down the unsuspecting victim within reach of their spiny mandibles.

BEETLES AND BUGS
Beetles

Few orders embody biological diversity quite like beetles (Coleoptera). Even accomplished entomologists only cautiously hazard a guess as to how many species exist worldwide: consensus is stuttering towards 370,000. Although beetles vary from tiny creatures best viewed with a magnifying glass to monsters bigger than your hand, all share a defining characteristic: hardened forewings (elytra) that protect soft hindwings.

Two Pantanal beetles attract attention by producing bioluminescence. Male fireflies (Lampyridae) attract females by flying slowly a metre above ground, pulsing green light from their abdomen. This light lacks ultraviolet rays so produces no heat – a highly energy-efficient process. The headlight click beetle (*Phyrophorus* sp.; Elateridae) emits two constant glows rather than one flashing light. Its genus name comes from the Greek for 'to bear fire'.

Scarab beetles (Scarabaeidae) have been revered by many societies for shiny elytra that gleam like precious metals. In the Pantanal, two less lustrous scarabs await. Green dung beetles (*Oxysternon palaemon*) are almost exclusively excrement-eaters, digging tunnels in which to store their faecal trophy. The other notable scarab is the elephant beetle (*Megasoma* sp.); the palm-sized male uses a forked horn as defence against rivals.

Bugs

While many people refer to virtually any insect as a 'bug', true bugs are members of the order Hemiptera. Hugely diverse, they range from tiny aphids (Aphididae) to giant water bugs (Belostomatidae) that include 12cm-long 'toe-biters' (*Lethocerus* sp.). Portentously named assassin bugs (Reduviidae) – identified by flattened bodies and black, white and red colouration – feed on blood; some transmit Chagas' disease, which afflicts ten million people in the Americas and is frequently fatal. Cicadas (Cicadidae) evoke awe for different reasons. Larvae live underground for years before emerging for a brief fortnight of adult existence when their sole goal is procreation. Males attract mates by vibrating a membrane in their resonant abdomen to emit a wrenchingly loud screech. The cicada cacophony eclipses even the background hum of orthopterans as the omnipresent Pantanal sound.

FLIES

Flies (Diptera) prop up a huge part of the Pantanal food chain, but many visitors may find it hard to appreciate their ecological value relative to their annoyance factor and role as disease vectors. Mosquitoes (Culicidae) are the greatest irritants, their incessant whine distracting even the most patient wildlife-watcher. Malaria, transmitted by nocturnal *Anopheles* mosquitoes, is not a particular problem in the Pantanal. However,

The screeching of male cicadas, produced by vibrating a membrane in their abdomen, can test your eardrums. (JL)

beware the day-flying *Aedes aegypti*, the vector for yellow and dengue fevers. Botflies (Oestridae) lay their eggs in live victims, either directly or via an intermediary such as a housefly (Muscidae). Body heat from the mammalian host prompts the egg to hatch, and the larva burrows under its host's skin where it remains until emergence. Most botflies parasitise cattle and deer (Cervidae), but the human botfly (*Dermatobia hominis*) prefers *Homo sapiens*. Turning from the gross to the enjoyable, however, hoverflies (Syrphidae) are a delight to watch. These insect helicopters hover inquisitively a few centimetres from your face before buzzing off to investigate another intriguing sight. Striped in black and yellow, hoverflies resemble stinging bees, a disguise that deters predators.

Hoverflies are frequently inquisitive, venturing within a few centimetres of your face; who is watching who? (JL)

BUTTERFLIES AND MOTHS

Butterflies are aerial jewels, their flashes of colour provoking gasps of wonder. Together with moths, they form the order Lepidoptera. Although many butterflies are vibrantly coloured and diurnal, and most moths dowdy and nocturnal, exceptions abound. For butterflies, reproduction is particularly demanding, and sperm production depletes the salt levels of many males. Mammal urine, faeces and sweat provide opportunities for mineral replenishment, so butterflies congregate in areas frequented by capybara. Stand still on a hot day, and a brave butterfly may even land on you to lap up your saline excretions.

Estimates of Pantanal butterfly diversity vary considerably, but there are probably more than 1,000 species in the Brazilian sector, one-third of the national tally. Less clear is the Pantanal proportion of Brazil's 23,000 moths. And even the most assiduous lepidopterist has yet to venture estimates for the Paraguayan and Bolivian sectors.

Grey crackers rest head-down on a tree, beautifully camouflaged. (JL)

The Nymphalidae are attractive butterflies; most have brightly coloured upperwings, but dull underwings that offer camouflage. Gulf fritillaries (*Agraulis vanillae*) fly powerfully, crossing large rivers with ease. Tyrant-flycatchers only make the mistake of catching a banded longwing (*Dryadula phaetusa*) once in their lives; this heliconiid is poisonous. When not perching upside down on a tree, superbly camouflaged, male grey crackers (*Hamadryas februa*) demarcate their territory with aggressive flights accompanied by a loud clicking (or 'cracking'). This sound is generated by the male striking together veins in its forewings –

The Illioneus giant owl is a butterfly so named for the owl-like 'eyes' on its hind underwing. (WP)

although entomologists once ascribed it to movement of the butterfly's genitalia! Larger nymphalids include two spectacular species. Concentric black and yellow circles stand out on the hind wing of the Illioneus giant owl (*Caligo illioneus*) – the resemblance to an owl's staring eye causing potential predators to backtrack. Equally stunning are morphos (*Morpho* sp.), huge creatures with iridescent blue patches on the upperwings that flap slowly through forest glades, each hefty wingbeat propelling the bearer upwards.

The Pieridae include several sociable butterflies. The great southern white (*Ascia monuste*) congregates in large numbers in midsummer, the effect recalling a snowstorm. The cloudless sulphur (*Phoebis sennae*) occurs in large lime-green flocks near rivers. Swallowtails (Papilionidae), such as *Hercalides* sp., are large and graceful, with long tail-like

Groups of graceful swallowtails (*Herclides* sp.) are a lovely Pantanal sight. (JL)

Eyemarks (*Mesosemia* sp.) are among many dazzling butterflies in Pantanal forests. (WP)

protrusions from their hindwings. The fast-flying Teleus longtail (*Urbanus teleus*) has a similar feature but is actually a spreadwing skipper (Hesperiidae).

Even experts can be flummoxed by moths, so most visitors content themselves with casual observations of obvious species. Hawk moths or sphinx moths (Sphingidae) are capable of sustained flight of up to 50km/h. The banded sphinx (*Eumorpha fasciata*) – its wings an alarming blaze of black, brown and pink – is common. All moths initiate the courtship process by secreting pheromones. Courting tiger moths (Arctiidae) go further, wooing prospective partners with a clicking sound. The closer the pair, the louder and more rapid the clicks.

Some termite species prefer to construct their remarkable nest above ground. (JL)

TERMITES

Tall cones of mud projecting above dry grasslands; mud ovals adorning large forest trees. Welcome to the colonial world of termites (order Isoptera), the oldest social insects on Earth. Each termite mound can house a million individuals divided into 'castes' – each with a body adapted to its specific role in the colony. Tiny workers forage and care for larvae. With large heads and jaws, soldiers defend the colony from attacks by anteaters. Queens dwarf their bodyguards and lay the colony's eggs, sometimes thousands per day.

A termite colony is both an architectural masterpiece and the nirvana of social organisation. Builders 5mm long construct the metre-tall mound, the human equivalent of building a 3km-high skyscraper. Below its sun-hardened surface, the mound contains numerous chambers, each with a specific purpose – food stores, egg nests, galleries replete with larvae and the queen's regal quarters. A remarkable ventilation system maintains constant temperature and humidity, expelling warm, stale air and admitting its cool, oxygen-rich replacement.

There are seven termite families and 2,750 species worldwide. Common Pantanal genera – *Nasutitermes* and *Amitermes* – are most obvious during mass emergences, which are most frequent after the first spring rains. Winged males and females take to the air to disperse, mate and establish new colonies. Many never live to fulfil these functions, instead being snared by grateful swallows.

ANTS, BEES AND WASPS

If you're rudely awoken from your Pantanal reverie by a sharp sting, the chances are that you have inadvertently threatened a female hymenopteran (order Hymenoptera). But look beyond your mild, temporary discomfort and you will find the most ecologically valuable insects on Earth. Ants (Formicidae) disperse seeds, recycle nutrients and aerate soil; bees (Apoidea) pollinate plants; and wasps (which span several superfamilies) control biological pests.

A trap-jaw ant can snap its jaws shut at 200km/h; watch where you put your fingers! (JL)

All are fascinating colonial creatures. Ant communities number millions of individuals that, like termites, are split into castes with distinct responsibilities. They have radiated to develop different niches; in Brazil alone, there are 2,500 species. Leafcutter ants (*Atta* or *Acromyrmex* sp.) denude vegetation around their colony, lines of ants scurrying nestwards waving squares of leaves – fodder for a fungus, which produces a spongy secretion that nourishes the ants. Burchell's army ants (*Eciton burchelli*; Ecitoninae) make swarming raids across the forest floor, hundreds of thousands of individuals devouring arthropods unfortunate enough to lie in their path. These marches attract antbirds to feed on

A mud-dauber wasp rolling a ball of mud, construction material for its lair. (JL)

invertebrates fleeing from the formicid predators. Another voracious predator is the trap-jaw ant (*Odontomachus* sp.), which opens its long mandibles 180 degrees and snaps them shut at 200km/h.

With perhaps half of Brazil's 3,000 species of bee, the Pantanal has plenty of pollinator potential. Stingless bees (Meliponini) are inexactly named; they have stings, albeit too rudimentary for defence. Highly social bees, meliponines produce honey – although seldom enough of it to make them worth cultivating. Orchid bees (Euglossini) are visually and ecologically distinctive; metallic green or blue, they are the only solitary pollen-carrying bees. Sweat bees (Halicitidae), meanwhile, are attracted to the salty skin of perspiring humans.

Wasps are less popular than bees, probably because their ecological contribution is less visible. Yet virtually every insect pest has a wasp that predates or parasitises it, and agriculturalists capitalise on these relationships. Parasitic wasps paralyse or kill an invertebrate and lay eggs in its comatose form or carcass. Spider wasps (Pompilidae) such as *Auplopus* are solitary species that sting a spider, then drag its paralysed form back to a nest burrow – no mean feat given that victim is larger than hunter. The wasp removes the spider's legs to prevent escape, then lays an egg on its abdomen, seals the burrow and departs. The larva hatches and feeds on the spider that – gruesomely – remains alive. Mud-daubers (*Sceliphron* sp.; Sphecidae) are long, slim wasps that roll up balls of mud to create a lair in which they store paralysed spiders. In one of nature's bittersweet ironies, mud-daubers are themselves often parasitised by cuckoo wasps (*Chrysis*).

Other wasps have a close relationship with plants – but in these instances the bond is two-way. Pollinating fig wasps (Agaoinidae) and their host fig trees (*Ficus* sp.) are a striking illustration of symbiosis. The tree allows wasps to use its fruit as egg chambers in exchange for pollination. Upon hatching, males have just two functions: first, to mate with females; second, to dig an escape tunnel so that females may escape to pollinate other trees.

ARACHNIDS

Arachnophobes have a fear of spiders (order Aranae), but the class Arachnida also includes other orders such as scorpions (Scorpiones), and ticks and mites (Acari). All have two body segments and four pairs of legs, differentiating them from insects, which have three of each.

Tangle-web spiders of the genus *Parawixia* are colonial, but only feed communally when prey is scarce. (JL)

SPIDERS

The Pantanal has at least 200 spiders, spread across 105 genera in 25 families. Two-thirds are in just three families: orb-web spiders (Araneidae), tangle-web spiders (Theridiidae) and jumping spiders (Salticidae). Orb-web spiders are master engineers, building circular, spiral-patterned webs of silk that serve as both home and snare. An insect lurching into the web is subdued by a bite then cocooned in silk. Genera such as *Mastophora* have an alternative approach: they are anglers. Bolas spiders secrete sticky globules infused with a pheromone and dangled on a single thread. The chemical entices male moths of particular species to approach – and get stuck, whereupon the spider reels in the line and feasts on its victim.

Three Pantanal tangle-web spider genera have contributed much to our understanding of arachnid life. Studies of widow spiders (*Latrodectus*) have examined their venom, silk and sexual biology (which includes cannibalism). *Anelosimus* spiders cover the spectrum from solitary to permanently social. *A. eximius* lives in colonies of a thousand individuals that occupy a basket-like web 3m in diameter and supported by threads extending 8m towards the canopy. Each spider builds, defends and feeds from its own section of the communal web. *Parawixia* spiders have a different take on this 'social yet solitary' approach to life, feeding alone except where prey is scarce or a large prey item is trapped, at which point they attack *en masse*.

The long-limbed brown huntsman spider keeps lodges free of cockroaches. (JL)

Worldwide, one arachnid in seven is a jumping spider. Pantanal genera include *Chira*, *Cotinusa* and *Thiodina*. All are capable of amazing jumping feats; by altering blood pressure and flow, jumping spiders extend their hind limbs to leap 50 times their body length, equivalent to a human bound of 75m. Rather like human BASE jumpers, they leap while attached by a safety line – in this case a silk thread.

Such tiny creatures are less worthy sources of fear than huntsman spiders (Sparassidae). The 13cm-long brown huntsman spider (*Heteropoda venatoria*) often startles visitors as it ambushes cockroaches (Blattodea) around lodge buildings. Scarier still in many people's eyes are tarantulas (Theraphosidae), giants of the spider world that crush victims with huge fangs then drool digestive juices over them. The chances of coming across one are low, however, as a recent Pantanal survey found only one hairy-legged species, *Acanthoscurria chacoana*, which is, in any case, harmless to humans.

SCORPIONS

The oldest of all arachnids and infamous for surviving long periods without food or water, scorpions have a literal 'sting in their tail'. When hunting or threatened, scorpions arch

A female scorpion (*Tityus* sp.) carries its offspring on its back. (CM/FLPA)

their tail forward over their body and prepare to strike with the venom-infused tip. The long, claw-like pincers are primarily for show, but prospective mates also use them to grapple one another in their twirling courtship dance. Although the sting of all scorpions is painful, only a low proportion of the world's 1,500–2000 species are venomous to humans. The poisonous few include several in the genus *Tityus*, famous for reproducing by parthenogenesis, a process whereby unfertilised eggs become living embryos. Several *Tityus* occur in the Pantanal: *T. confluens* is typical of drier areas. Despite their notoriety, scorpions remain poorly known: in the year 2000, arachnologists described an entirely new genus (*Brazilobothriurus*) from the Pantanal.

TICKS AND MITES

Ticks are one tiny arthropod that most visitors hope not to encounter while wandering Pantanal grasslands. They and other mites (order Acari) survive by gorging on the blood of mammals and birds. Ticks (Ixodidae) wait on grass stems until they detect heat from a passing host, whereupon they hitch a ride and imbed jaws in the victim. Beneath rigid dorsal plates, their soft, flexible abdomens expand as they imbibe. Ticks are vectors for several diseases, including Lyme disease.

CENTIPEDES, SNAILS AND CRUSTACEANS

The remaining noteworthy Pantanal invertebrates fall into three evolutionarily separate groups. Centipedes and millipedes (class Myriapoda) and crustaceans (superclass Crustacea) are all arthropods in the phylum Arthropoda, but snails (class Gastropoda) are members of a separate phylum, the molluscs (Mollusca).

CENTIPEDES AND MILLIPEDES

Centipedes (class Chilopoda) and millipedes (Diplopoda) have more appendages than insects by an order or two of magnitude. Lacking a waterproof cuticle, these terrestrial arthropods inhabit humid microhabitats in moist forests. Millipedes have hundreds of legs

Millipedes curl up to reduce their vulnerability to predators. (JL)

(but never thousands, as their name suggests) and chunter slowly through leaf litter, munching decomposing plant matter or rolling into a ball should they sense danger. Compared with millipedes, centipedes have a single pair (rather than two) of longer legs on each body segment. This enables them to move quickly, as befits an aggressive carnivore with venomous claws that pack a killer punch.

In the dry season, red freshwater crabs move across arid terrain in search of wetlands. (JL)

CRUSTACEANS

The size spectrum of crustaceans (superclass Crustacea) ranges from water fleas (Clacodera) to lobsters (Nephropidae). Almost all are aquatic. In the Pantanal, the most notable are shrimps (Palaemonidae, Sergestidae) and crabs (Trichodactylidae). Typical inhabitants of lowland rivers and wetlands, they play important roles at different trophic levels, being herbivores, predators, decomposers and prey for other groups. Shrimps are important fodder for carnivorous fish; the Pantanal hosts three members of the genus *Macrobrachium*, the most common being the Amazon river prawn *M. amazonicum*, a candidate for commercial farming. Of the seven crabs, visitors are most likely to encounter the red freshwater crab *Dilocarcinus pagei* as it wanders roads between dwindling water bodies. Such manoeuvres are risky, and many end up in the gullet of a snail kite.

SNAILS

Snails (order Gastropoda) play an important role in the Pantanal ecosystem. These and other 'zoobenthos' that feed on algae and microorganisms serve as important prey for fish, mammals such as the South American coati, and birds such as the limpkin. The most common snail is the aquatic apple snail (*Pomacea guyanensis*); empty shells are a frequent sight beneath perches used by snail kites.

A shell is all that remains of this aquatic apple snail, its former occupant eaten by a snail kite or limpkin. (JL)

WHERE TO GO

The Transpantaneira highway
in Mato Grosso, Brazil. (JL)

From a visitor's perspective, the Pantanal falls into four areas. This chapter considers each in terms of where to look for wildlife, where to stay and how to get around. Whichever area you choose, the Pantanal merits a very minimum of three nights. The longer your trip the more cost-effective, since accommodation is expensive and budget travel difficult.

Both the two main areas are in Brazil. In the north, the Transpantaneira highway of Mato Grosso state provides access to varied habitat and a score of lodges; it is ideal for a multi-venue trip of one to two weeks. To the south, the cities of Campo Grande,

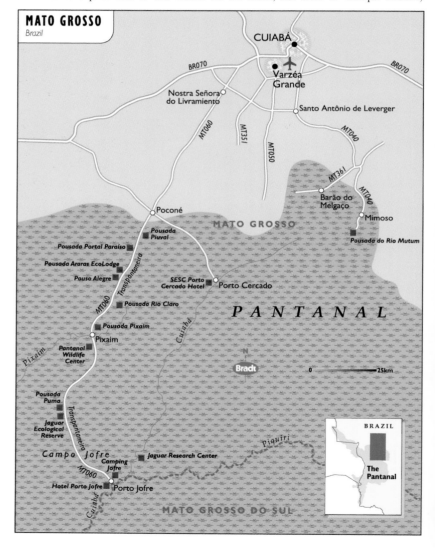

Aquidauana and Miranda in Mato Grosso do Sul are departure points for several decent lodges that are widely separated and less easy to combine. To the west, those on a tight budget (see box on page 136, *Pantanal on the cheap?*) should consider an intrepid adventure into the little-disturbed Bolivian Pantanal of Santa Cruz province – in preference to the unimpressive operations based in adjacent Corumbá across the Brazilian border. At its southern limit, the Pantanal scrapes into Paraguay, where two remote lodges have great potential.

MATO GROSSO, BRAZIL

The Transpantaneira is the only road to penetrate deep into the Pantanal. Constructed in 1976 to link the cities of Cuiabá in Mato Grosso and Corumbá in Mato Grosso do Sul, the road extends south from the small town of Poconé only as far as Porto Jofre on the Cuiabá River, 148km and more than 120 wooden bridges later, and thus ends hundreds of kilometres short of its intended destination. Lodges identify their location in terms of distance along the road. Many visitors make a pit stop in Poconé, where information, internet facilities and last-minute bookings are available.

The Transpantaneira is excellent for wildlife-watching. During the dry season, roadside ditches created when building the road retain water so become a magnet for waterbirds, mammals, reptiles and amphibians. Moreover, the road crosses a wide range of habitats: dry grasslands and open scrub in the north gradually give way to large semi-deciduous forests and extensive swamps. This habitat gradient means that each lodge along the road has its own distinctive wildlife offering: there is little point looking for a jaguar in the north, and ditto a giant anteater in the south. It thus makes sense to stay at three or more widely separated lodges: there is easily enough excitement for one to two weeks.

Also in Mato Grosso, a cheaper alternative is the Barão de Melgaço area, southeast of Poconé. Core wildlife is similar to that on the Transpantaneira, but there is less chance of seeing jaguar.

The official entrance to the Transpantaneira; prepare for 150km of widlife-watching. (JL)

Ringed kingfishers find rich pickings in the waterways alongside the Transpantaneira. (JL)

WILDLIFE HOTSPOTS AND ACCOMMODATION

The season – and its associated water levels – decrees how soon along the Transpantaneira you start seeing the throngs of waterbirds that characterise the Pantanal. Roadside ditches teem with egrets (great and snowy), herons (striated and rufescent tiger), ibises (green and buff-necked) and storks (American wood and jabiru). In the air, kites (snail and plumbeous) sail over marshy terrain replete with prey. Kingfishers (ringed, amazon and green, in descending order of size) use telegraph wires as a vantage point for their piscatorial activities. Below them, capybara families graze while hawks (roadside and black-collared) search for invertebrates from posts. Careful perusal of the shallows should reveal the eyes and nostrils of your first yacaré caiman – and then another, and another… Freshly arrived visitors may find it hard to drag themselves away from this first spectacle, but many more such opportunities await, particularly off-road in *fazendas* (ranches) that offer lodging.

Transpantaneira bridges are for birds as well as birders. (JL)

The first such fazenda is **Pousada Piuval**, *(20 rooms; tel: +55 65 3345 1338 [reservations] or +55 65 3345 2545 [lodge]; email: reservas@pousadapiuval.com.br; www.pousadapiuval.com.br; open all year. US$180 pp sharing, inc FB, transfers, local guide & activities)*, 3km east of the Transpantaneira at km10. This 7,000ha cattle ranch has been in the Eubank family for 150 years and, in 2009, celebrated its 20th anniversary of catering for ecotourists. Eduardo Eubank, the attentive manager, is proud of the low environmental impact management systems that he has introduced: most hot water is solar-heated, batteries are recycled and lighting is motion-activated. Outdated décor is lifted by vibrant local artwork, and the well-designed outside space includes fireside seating, a children's play area and an attractive swimming pool. A souvenir shop caters to the acquisitive, satellite television to the square-eyed, and free Wi-Fi to email junkies.

Piuval offers an impressive array of fauna and flora. The word *piuval* means 'place with many *piuva*', the lapacho tree that splashes vivid pink across the spring forest. A 20-seater converted lorry transports visitors around a mosaic of grassland and woodlots interspersed with permanent water bodies. In the dry season, those with a 4x4 may drive off-track, enabling photographers to sidle up to birds such as greater rhea and nacunda nighthawk. Alternatively, you can bike, ride or walk along three long trails. These paths offer good birding as forest islands hold

After a hot morning's wildlife-watching, cool off in the pristine pool at Pousada Piuval.

sought-after creatures such as chestnut-bellied guan, bare-faced curassow, white-lored spinetail, dull-capped attila, planalto slaty-antshrike and Mato Grosso antbird. It is hard not to see hyacinth macaw, as several breeding pairs munch on *buriti* palm nuts. At night, head out for puma, both anteaters and Azara's night monkey – the last difficult to see elsewhere along the Transpantaneira.

Alternatively, take a boat trip around the *baía* (large bay) for close views of storks, herons, ibises and other waterbirds, such as least bittern and southern screamer. Or pause in gallery forest for mammals such as black-tailed marmoset and black howler, plus birds such as red-billed scythebill and buff-bellied hermit. On dry land, a tower gives panoramic views over an egret and stork colony; search nearby permanent water bodies for yellow anaconda and large groups of yacaré.

The grasslands of the northern Transpantaneira are good habitat for greater rheas. (JL)

Pousada Portal Paraíso (*10 rooms plus camping; tel: +55 65 3345 2271; email: portalparaiso@vsp.com.br; www.portalparaiso.com.br; open all year. US$100 pp sharing, inc FB & transfers. Activities extra*) lies immediately west of the Transpantaneira at km17. Accommodation and board are considerably cheaper than other lodges, camping rates are a bargain and pick-up from Poconé is free. For those on a tight schedule as well as budget, there is even a day-rate. The lodge is attractively designed in dark wood; the cute bar bordering the swimming pool presides over grasslands that hold greater rhea and southern tamandua. The 870ha property boasts three pairs of hyacinth macaws, one nesting just 100m from the lodge. Visitors explore by walking on forest trails; arrange trained wildlife guides in advance. Visitors may also hire bicycles or horses, or take an inexpensive two-hour night safari. Motorboat and canoes, moored on the nearby Claro River, can be hired at reasonable rates of US$95 for a full day.

At km32, west of the road, is **Pousada Araras EcoLodge** (*19 rooms; tel: +55 65 3682 2800 [reservations] or +55 65 9998 4781 [lodge]; email: reservas@araraslodge.com.br; www.araraslodge.com.br; open all year. US$200 pp sharing, inc FB, transfers, bilingual wildlife guide, boat trip & night safari*). Charismatic owner André Von Thuronyi, son of a Hungarian nobleman and pioneer of Pantanal tourism, provides a warm welcome. Rustic yet sophisticated, the lodge is attractive and well maintained. Innovative use of local materials and foodstuffs (such as a delicious dessert of green papaya and cane juice) create a homely and intimate feel, and the availability of reflexology and craniology sessions is in keeping with the relaxed ambience. But Araras is

Access to Transpantaneira forests is occasionally by boardwalk as well as footpath. (JL)

Black howlers – here a young male – tend to feed quietly in the forest canopy. (JL)

more than a place to unwind; its 3,000 hectares are packed with wildlife. In Portuguese, *arara* means 'macaw', and a pair of hyacinth macaws nests 20m from the breakfast veranda, sharing a tree with great horned owls and roosting lesser bulldog and Pallas's mastiff bats. Habituated capybara wander around the gardens; one day, a puma was observed hunting them.

Knowledgeable, English-speaking guides escort visitors to the best wildlife sites. An elevated boardwalk enters good-quality forest, and is regularly used by an ocelot as well as humans. Bird specialities such as white-lored spinetail, band-tailed antbird, Mato Grosso antbird and helmeted manakin are easily seen. The boardwalk runs past a pool that entices thirsty South American tapir. This area is good for black-tailed marmoset, Azara's agouti and, at night, grey four-eyed opossum.

Just 1km from the lodge, a tower offers a superb panoramic view over seasonally flooded wetland and drier grassland. A black howler troop roosts on the tower, offering close views at dawn and dusk. Below, look for treats such as capped heron amidst plentiful waterbirds. Marsh deer and feral pigs graze peacefully nearby, while yacaré loiter. Lucky visitors have seen jaguar – rare this far north – and giant anteater. From the tower, a trail extends through sandy scrub – a good place for nine-banded armadillo, South American coati, black-striped tufted capuchin and bare-faced curassow.

The property extends east of the Transpantaneira into the Passo do Ema, where dry grasslands offer a great chance of both anteaters. Night drives usually encounter both brocket deer, tapeti and crab-eating raccoon. You can also explore on horseback. Trails lead through dry forests with tayra, black howler and black-tailed marmoset. Boat trips from Baía dos Ciervos on Clarinho River are good for both otters, sungrebe and agami heron. Some visitors stay overnight here in a basic tented riverside camp or in the pretty guesthouse at Pasa Diama.

Heading south, you immediately pass a small café under the lodge's ownership. **Barara** offers a shady retreat with revitalising drinks and snacks. Keep an ear out for hyacinth macaw and white woodpecker. If you're not staying at the EcoLodge, you can make arrangements here to visit its boardwalk.

One kilometre south, at km33, is **Pouso Alegre**. *(13 rooms; tel: +55 65 626 1545 [reservations] or +55 65 9968 6101 [lodge]; email: alegre.p@terra.com.br; www.pousalegre.com.br; open all year. US$65 pp sharing, inc FB, local guide & activities).* This cattle ranch is excellent for wildlife. The bumpy entrance track is used by brocket deer, crab-eating fox, South American coati, chestnut-bellied guan and bare-faced curassow. Wait by secluded water

A rare daytime view of the aptly named boat-billed heron. (HP)

hollows to see what fancies a drink: capped heron, green ibis and sunbittern are all likely. Just 1km before the lodge, an elevated embankment crosses open grassland. Scan from here, particularly at dawn and dusk: South American tapir is regular, and greater rhea and red-legged seriema stroll around.

Lodge manager Luis Vicente Campos, a herpetologist, has compiled a mouth-watering catalogue of fauna and flora found in Alegre's 11,000ha of varied habitat. Mammalian highlights include giant armadillo and bush dog, both so rare as to be near-mythical. Alegre's 35 species of snake include yellow anaconda, Brazilian redtail boa and common tiger ratsnake. Among 310 bird species are 13 parrots, seven owls, 11 woodpeckers and 16 hummingbirds. The 550 species of plant identified include members of 100 families.

Luis has trained the ranch's *peões* to show visitors wildlife on foot or horseback along trails. South American tapir and southern tamandua occur within 200m of the lodge, and giant anteater often within 500m. Black-tailed marmoset and black howler inhabit gallery forests along the Bento Gomes River. Permanent wetlands are the best place to see marsh deer; pampas deer also occurs. Six species of cat have been recorded, but all are very rare: there's no realistic chance of jaguar.

Large trees provide the lodge with respite from the searing sun. Rooms are large and simple; most have air conditioning. Good food is served in a large restaurant decorated with local artwork. Even while taking a siesta on the shady balcony, you can't get away from wildlife. Yellow-billed cardinals are abundant and hyacinth macaws roost within earshot, while a crab-eating fox trots up to the kitchen each evening, waiting for scraps.

As you head further south along the Transpantaneira, stay alert for wildlife. During the day, South American coati, marsh deer and tayra may cross at any time, while roadside trees hold interesting birds such as peach-fronted parakeet and crimson-crested woodpecker. This area is great for night drives: crab-eating fox, crab-eating raccoon, southern tamandua and three species of deer are regular. Lucky visitors may chance upon South American tapir, giant anteater or ocelot. If mammals aren't co-operating, scrutinise roadside ditches for a boat-billed heron among the crowd of black-crowned night-herons.

At km63, the Transpantaneira crosses the Pixaim River, which marks a distinct change in soil and vegetation. Southwards, red earth predominates and the stony road is replaced by a slippery surface. Forests become larger and denser, and wetlands more frequent and extensive. Among accommodation options here, the grandly named **Pantanal Wildlife Center** (*10 rooms; tel: +55 65 3682 3175; email: sales@pantanalwildlifecenter.com; www.pantanalwildlifecenter.com; closed 23 Dec–1 Jan. US$200 pp sharing, inc FB, activities & bilingual wildlife guide. Transfers extra*) – also known by its original, more prosaic name of **Fazenda Santa Teresa** – stands out for wildlife enthusiasts.

Early morning boat trips along rivers are an integral part of the Pantanal experience. (HP)

Just south of the river, head west along the bumpy entrance track for 3km to the lodge. Owned by wildlife conservationist and entrepreneur Charlie Munn, the lodge's slick website creates high expectations. Although not quite all it promises is actually delivered, the Pantanal Wildlife Center is still very good, with several features setting it apart from most competitors. Innovations such as movable observation towers enable visitors to enjoy intimate insights into nesting jabiru and great potoo. A boon for photographers, an electric catamaran is sometimes available for noise-free river trips, although most excursions are in motorboats. Five kilometres of trails lead through gallery forest, drier woodland and scrub. A feeding platform attracts hyacinth macaws. Knowledgeable, bilingual wildlife guides use mp3 players to attract skulking birds. Note, however, that activities are conducted in groups of up to nine, so you may be lumped together with others.

Giant otters are a highlight of the River Pixaim. Formerly co-operative, groups have moved farther from the lodge and can be difficult to find. While searching, check out shady vegetation for zigzag and agami herons. Sungrebes often hide in water hyacinths, common iguanas adorn overhanging branches and rusty-backed spinetails flit across the water.

Either side of the lodge, trails enter dense gallery forest. The eastern trail leads through the territory of a semi-habituated group of black-striped tufted capuchin; black-tailed marmoset and black howler are also regular. All the Pantanal's forest bird specialities are present. In scrub, look for pampas

Look for giant otters along the River Pixaim. (JL)

Great horned owl occurs widely in the Pantanal; look for roosting birds or listen for them at dusk. (JL)

deer, buff-bellied hermit, white-naped xenopsaris and rusty-backed antwren. The Pantanal Wildlife Center shares an open-sided safari vehicle with other lodges. When available, this can be used for night drives. The entrance track is very good for South American tapir and southern tamandua. Ocelot and giant anteater regularly commute along the adjacent Transpantaneira.

Even the lodge gardens are packed with wildlife. Flowering trees attract orange-backed troupial, chestnut-eared araçari and various hummingbirds. Yellow-billed cardinals and giant cowbirds gorge on leftovers. Great horned owl and crab-eating fox are regular nocturnal visitors. And what can be better than lounging in a hammock, sipping an evening beer and watching the aerial foraging of bulldog bats and nighthawks? The accommodation is simple but attractive, and the airy restaurant includes a cosy seating area stocked with wildlife books.

Other accommodation options around Pixaim do not offer quite such impressive wildlife-watching – although there is, of course, wildlife everywhere. Just north of the river bridge at km62, **Pousada Pixaim** (*10 rooms; tel: +55 65 3664 3718 [reservations] or +55 65 3345 2091 [lodge]; email: atendimento@pousadapixaim.com.br; www.queenofthe pantanal.com; open Mar–Dec; US$50 pp sharing, FB; activities extra*) was one of the first Pantanal lodges and merits mention on account of its cheapness. Small bedrooms are spartan but clean, and the restaurant has character, being built on stilts over a wetland that South American tapir sometimes visits. Wildlife-watching facilities are few, but visitors may hire boats and horses, or walk two trails through forest with black-tailed marmoset and helmeted manakin. River trips should encounter a similar selection of species to that listed for the Pantanal Wildlife Center.

South of Pixaim there is no accommodation for 35km. Wildlife interest along this stretch is relatively limited, although roadside ditches hold waterbirds, yacaré and capybara, and mammals and lizards may cross the road at any moment. Birders examining roadside scrub and woodland should find insectivores such as buff-breasted and moustached wrens, rusty-fronted tody-flycatcher and ashy-headed greenlet.

Shortly after the 100km mark, two lodges appear in quick succession, their feline names announcing that we are now entering cat-spotting territory. The first is **Pousada Puma** (*16 rooms; tel: +55 65 3345 3528 [reservations] or +55 65 9901 9801 [lodge]; no email or website; open all year, although Transpantaneira often impassable. US$60 pp sharing inc FB, local guide, bicycle & walks; boat trip extra unless staying 2 nights*) at km106, a 700ha property that comprises mainly forest accessed via trails. Visitor facilities – a basic camp and observation tower – are under construction deep in the forest. Pousada Puma's wildlife is little known, but both hyacinth macaws and jabiru breed. You can easily see black howler and black-striped tufted capuchin in the forest, and have reasonable chances of jaguar, ocelot and South American tapir along the adjacent Transpantaneira. There is no river so the lodge's boat is moored on the Cuiabá River near Porto Jofre, 42km south. Inexpensive accommodation is brightly coloured and adorned with bold artwork, though bedrooms currently lack air conditioning and electricity is available only in the evening.

A better option is **Jaguar Ecological Reserve** (*9 rooms; tel: +55 65 3636 8557 [reservations] or +55 65 9958 4306 [mobile]; email: rejaguar@bol.com.br; www.jaguarreserve.com; open all year. US$200 pp sharing, inc FB, transfers, boat trips, bilingual wildlife guide & all activities*) at km110. The co-owner/manager, Eduardo Falcão de Arruda, is a bilingual wildlife guide who happily works long hours to show visitors wildlife. Formerly known as Pousada Pantaneira, the Focus Conservation Fund helped create the 1,200ha reserve in 1999. Profits are reinvested in land acquisition to extend protection of semi-deciduous forest and scrub. Although the lodge's name should not be taken as a guarantee, jaguars are regular along the Transpantaneira (lying on the road in the car-free summer!), and there is no better area for ocelot.

South American tapirs are sometimes seen swimming between riverbanks. (JL)

Wildlife-watching is very good. Hyacinth macaws are common around the *acuri* palms and several pairs breed. Trails enter the forest behind the lodge and opposite the turn-off to Santa Isabel at km112; most Pantanal bird specialities occur. The derelict research centre buildings, 300m along the Santa Isabel road, are good for wildlife. Great potoo occurs, along with black-banded, spectacled and ferruginous pygmy-owls. Yellow-collared and hyacinth macaws gather in late afternoons. South American tapir and red brocket are regular, and Seba's short-tailed bats roost in an abandoned hut. Black-tailed marmoset and lowland paca occur further along the Santa Isabel road. Back towards the Jaguar Ecological Reserve, look for giant otter, boat-billed heron and all five kingfishers from the first bridge south of the lodge.

The beady-eyed maguari stork is a speciality of Campo Jofre (see page 131). (JL)

Eduardo uses an open-top safari truck for diurnal and nocturnal safaris. The three main diurnal primates, crab-eating raccoon, nine-banded armadillo and Neotropical otter are often seen. Regular reptiles include caiman lizard and yellow-tailed cribo. Heller's broad-nosed and Pallas's mastiff bats roost around the lodge. The property lacks rivers, so Eduardo moors his boat near Porto Jofre, 37km to the south and runs river trips from there to look for jaguar.

Accommodation is more basic than at some lodges, though meals are generous and the well-designed bedrooms feature some interesting touches, such as mirror frames with bird carvings. Visitors who value their creature comforts will be pleased to know that three deluxe chalets and a swimming pool are under construction as this book goes to press.

Heading south, the remaining 35km of the Transpantaneira offer great potential for memorable wildlife encounters. Traffic is light, so mammals and reptiles treat the road as their own, particularly if surrounding vegetation is wet. Roadside woodland and scrub are good for birding. A couple of bridges host roosting proboscis bats. The key area is Campo Jofre, a vast wetland that extends for several kilometres after km127. The area heaves with herons, egrets, limpkins, ibises and storks: the star bird is maguari stork, common here but rare further north. Large trees around an abandoned research station offer shade and shelter, notably for great horned owl. After a hot day, the warm road is a good place to search for yellow anaconda, Mato Grosso lancehead and smaller snakes such as common water liophis.

Leaving Campo Jofre, you enter the final 10km of the Transpantaneira. From bridges, scan for marsh deer, Neotropical otter and sungrebe. Jaguar and ocelot are often seen on night drives. One kilometre before the Cuiabá River, at km146, a rutted track heads left to **Camping Jofre** (*12 tent pitches; tel: +55 65 3661 4703 or +55 65 8403 3620; email: portojofrepantanal@terra.com.br; US$7 pp, meals extra*). Brazilian fishermen are the main users of the area's only budget accommodation. The riverside location is great, though comes loaded with mosquitoes. Washrooms, toilet blocks and a simple restaurant supplement shady tent pitches. Azara's agouti, a hyacinth macaw nest and rufous cacholotes provide wildlife interest. For river trips, ask the imposing manager, Oscar, to arrange boats from the nearby Pesqueiro Comê Agua.

Plumbeous ibis prefers secluded, muddy areas such as the lagoon behind Hotel Porto Jofre. (JL)

Hotel Porto Jofre (*26 rooms; tel: +55 65 3637 1593/1263; email: contato@portojofre.com.br; www.portojofre.com.br; open Mar–Oct. US$110 pp sharing, FB. Boat hire and transfers extra*) lies at the end of the Transpantaneira (km147). Slickly run by the irrepressible Gustavo Santos, this large, attractive and well-designed hotel targets wealthy

A quiet tributary of the Cuiabá River, ideal habitat for giant otter and sungrebe. (JL)

Brazilian fishermen but also caters for wildlife tour groups, attracted by its location on the Cuiabá River. Bedrooms are modern and spacious. Facilities include a swimming pool, games room and airstrip. A large restaurant serves good food, and service is excellent. Almost uniquely, Porto Jofre routinely offers an early breakfast, enabling a dawn start on the river when activity is greatest and where the goal is jaguar.

The Cuiabá east of Porto Jofre is undoubtedly the best place to see this magnificent feline anywhere in its range. Sharp-eyed boat drivers know the area well. Chances are better further from Porto Jofre; the key area is *Tres irmãos* ('Three brothers'), one hour away. Another good area is the Piquiri River. While lucky visitors have seen jaguars within a few minutes of Porto Jofre, the dedicated cat enthusiast should maximise chances by spending three or more days on the river. The hotel has 35 boats; prices for full-day hire range from US$200 (small motorised canoe) to US$925 (ten-seater motorboat).

There is plenty to enjoy while searching for jaguar. Chances of both otters are high in both *Tres irmãos* and the Piquiri. Black howlers, hyacinth macaws and sometimes South American tapir forage along riverbanks. Pied lapwings scuttle past black skimmers and terns along open sandbanks. In quieter stretches of narrow rivers beyond *Tres irmãos*, look for sunbittern, sungrebe, bare-faced curassow and common iguana. All five kingfishers and rufous-tailed jacamar perch on overhanging branches, and boisterous black-capped donacobius scold from dense aquatic vegetation. As dusk falls, the air fills with band-tailed nighthawks and both bulldog bats. At night, train a spotlight on the riverbank for ocelot.

Back on land, the area around Porto Jofre is also good, although this is not a wildlife *pousada* like those elsewhere on the Transpantaneira. Behind the hotel, a lagoon strewn with giant waterlilies (native to the western Pantanal and presumably introduced here) provides habitat for southern screamer, maguari stork and plumbeous ibis. Hyacinth macaws visit the hotel complex each day, often drinking from the water tower; a gimmicky macaw-shaped phone booth honours their presence. It is well worth birding the rough triangle formed by the hotel, campsite and the junction at km146 on the Transpantaneira, where highlights include 'lekking' cinnamon-throated hermits, chestnut-bellied guan, little cuckoo, golden-green woodpecker and moustached wren.

Those with deep pockets wishing the ultimate in jaguar tourism should base themselves in the heart of the big cat's Pantanal territory at the **Jaguar Research Center** (*8 walk-in tents; tel: +55 65 3682 3175; email reservas@pantanalwildlifecenter.com; www.jaguarresearchcenter.com; closed 23 Dec–1 Jan. US$790 pp sharing, inc FB, all boat trips, bilingual wildlife guide & transfers from Pantanal Wildlife Center*). Under the same ownership as the Pantanal Wildlife Center, this lodge takes its cue from Africa's luxury tented-safaris. Superbly situated amidst the *Tres irmãos* river complex, accommodation comprises spacious walk-in tents with stylish décor (jaguar-print cushions!), wooden floors and electricity. Managers and guests alike work hard to minimise adverse environmental impacts: visitors take bush showers and use dry 'ecological' toilets.

Wildlife gimmicks are common in the Pantanal; should one laugh or cry? (JL)

Good meals are taken on an air-conditioned twin-deck houseboat, with a great river view.

Wildlife is as listed for the Cuiabá River under Hotel Porto Jofre above. However, the difference is that all activities aim to maximise chances of seeing jaguar. Scout boats depart in different directions at dawn. Should a jaguar be spotted, boats share the location by radio to give everyone equal opportunity to enjoy the spectacle. The small size of the operation means that there are never more than a couple of boats at any one animal, and boatmen hold off at a respectful distance. With such concerted investment, it is unsurprising that success rates are high. In the first three months of the 2008 season, there were 105 jaguar encounters. There is even the unnerving prospect of bumping into a jaguar around camp; animals pass through each night, so guests are prohibited from walking alone.

Search the banks of the Cuiabá River for jaguar. (JL)

As the lodge's name suggests, resident biologists conduct jaguar research. Studies reveal that there are up to 26 jaguars in the area, each individually identifiable by the pattern of dark marks on its head. The calculated density of three to four animals per 100km^2 is far higher than elsewhere in the jaguar's range. As these findings have not yet been published, however, rival operators have mischievously suggested that the primary aim of the 'research' is to inform efforts to show jaguars to tourists. Perhaps they're just jealous.

A group of happy jaguar-watchers returning to Porto Jofre. (JL)

Away from the Transpantaneira but still in Mato Grosso is the **Barão de Melgaço**. This area caters primarily to Brazilian residents, particularly fishermen, and there is less emphasis on wildlife-watching. There are fewer options for a varied multi-venue trip. Nevertheless, a couple of lodges may be worth considering as a complement to your Transpantaneira trip, particularly because they tend to be cheaper.

SESC Porto Cercado Hotel (*108 rooms; tel: +55 65 3688 2001/2005; email: reservas@sescpantanal.com.br or sescpantanal06@terra.com.br; www.sescpantanal.com.br; open all year. From US$75 pp sharing, FB. Transfers, guide & activities extra*) lies 45km southeast of Poconé along the unpaved MT370. This road can be good for greater rhea and blue-and-yellow macaw; jaguar and ocelot are occasionally seen crossing the road. The hotel adjoins a 106,000ha reserve that includes gallery forest, cerrado and seasonally inundated grassland. Four trails run through semi-deciduous woodland, one leading to an observation tower. The usual interesting Pantanal passerines occur, as does chestnut-bellied guan along the reserve road. You may hire boats to explore the Cuiabá River and bays north towards the Barão de Melgaço, where there is a good chance of giant otter and black howler. Puma and maned wolf occur in the reserve, as does jaguar in the wetter western section. In 2009, a harpy eagle nest was discovered in the reserve. The state-run hotel is luxurious by Pantanal standards, but lacks the charm of traditional establishments. Bedrooms are well equipped and there is a large restaurant serving tasty food. For visitors craving a break from wildlife-watching, sports and children's facilities abound; there is even a conference centre.

With a beautiful setting in the east of the Baía de Santa Mariana, **Pousada do Rio Mutum** *(22 rooms; tel: +55 65 3052 7022; email: pousadamutum @pousadamutum.com.br; www.pousadamutum.com.br; open all year. US$100pp sharing, inc FB. Activities extra)* is the best-known lodge around Barão de Melgaço. Its cottage-like accommodation is stylish, and the large circular restaurant feels surprisingly intimate. Carved wood abounds, and hammocks are slung under mango trees and around a swimming pool amidst attractive gardens. Rio Mutum is the most wildlife-focused of the area's establishments – although less so than most Transpantaneira lodges. Visitors can arrange night safaris, horserides and walks along several trails. Alternatively, head by motorboat into Sia Mariana or Chacororé bays for giant otter and black howlers. Most Pantanal bird specialities occur in the vicinity, including chestnut-bellied guan, agami and zigzag herons, sungrebe, sunbittern, hyacinth macaw and planalto slaty-antshrike.

Transport

Cuiabá provides the gateway to Mato Grosso's Pantanal. Visitors usually arrive by bus at Cuiabá or by plane at the airport in adjacent Varzéa Grande. Most lodges offer transfers. Alternatively, local wildlife travel agencies usually include a vehicle and driver/guide in their packages. Most visitors plump for one of these two options.

Visitors wanting more flexibility or intending to visit a variety of lodges would do well to hire a vehicle. Of the international companies, Avis *(tel: +55 65 3682 6630; www.avis.com)*, Hertz *(tel: +55 65 3682 8005; www.hertz.com)* and Localiza *(tel: +55 65 3682 7900; www.localiza.com)* have airport offices. Local companies at the airport or in town include Alfa *(tel: +55 65 3634 0300; www.alfarentacar.com.br)*, Atlanta *(tel: +55 65 3685 2882; www.atlantarentacar.com.br)* and Easy *(tel: +55 65 3052 0210; www.easyrentacar.com.br)*. Cars start from around US$200 per week; expect to pay four times that for a 4x4.

During the dry season, a saloon car is usually sufficient provided that it does not rain. Should it do so, the Transpantaneira (particularly south of the Pixaim River) turns into slithery porridge, caking wheels with mud and impeding driving. Drive cautiously and make provision for delays.

Drive cautiously across the Transpantaneira's 120 bridges *(above)*, but don't forget to look for loitering sunbitterns *(below)*. (JL)

The same advice applies to Transpantaneira bridges. Most are wooden and, while now in reasonable condition, need careful navigation: bridges in the south frequently lack the odd plank. Petrol is scarce along the Transpantaneira. Distances are short, but the average speed of 30km/h and frequent wildlife stops lead to low fuel efficiency. Fill up in Poconé; options thereafter are limited. Pousada Pixaim and Hotel Porto Jofre have petrol pumps, but these are often empty; Oscar at Camping Jofre sells petrol at a considerable mark-up. In an emergency, be prepared to pay over the odds to persuade a lodge to relinquish some of its fiercely guarded supply.

PANTANAL ON THE CHEAP?

On a tight budget it is hard to be sure of a good Pantanal experience because accommodation is almost universally expensive in the Brazilian Pantanal. In Mato Grosso, however, you could do worse than bus to Poconé, from where Pousada Portal Paraíso (page 124) offers a free transfer to its lodge at km17 on the Transpantaneira. Camping is cheap, even with full board; hire a bike to see great wildlife spectacles along the road. Among the lodges, Pouso Alegre (page 125) and Pousada Pixaim (page 128) offer the cheapest beds, and you can camp beside the Cuiabá River at Camping Jofre (page 131) – though you'll need to hire a car with some of the money saved on accommodation. The truly thrifty could go further and –

Lodges are sometimes adorned with local artwork or other decorations. (JL)

factoring in long waits – hitch along the Transpantaneira, and save their money to rent a boat to search for jaguar. Away from the Transpantaneira, SESC Porto Cercado Hotel (page 134) offers cheap transfers from Cuiabá, and the adjacent reserve offers good wildlife-watching.

There are cheap but less rewarding options in Mato Grosso do Sul. Backpackers have tended to use Corumbá, 400km west of Campo Grande, as a base. From here, a plethora of guides and companies hawk their services to fresh arrivals. All promise much but many deliver little. Accommodation is usually on basic *fazendas* with few facilities, and you take pot luck as to the quality of wildlife-watching. You should see capybaras, yacarés, plenty of waterbirds and probably hyacinth macaw. But your chances of seeing true specialities – such as jaguar, giant otter and some of the less obtrusive birds – are remote.

The Pantanal is not blessed with public transport, and the Mato Grosso section is no exception. Buses run between Cuiabá and Poconé six times daily (US$6) and a taxi covering the same route costs anything from US$40 upwards. Along the Transpantaneira, however, there is nothing. The budget traveller's only options are to hitch (no safety problems reported, but long waits are likely) or pay for a lodge transfer.

For lodges east of Barão de Melgaço, drive south from Cuiabá along the paved MT040 to Santo Antônio do Leverger, 70km along an unpaved road to Mimoso, then a further 13km to the Mutum River bridge. Pousada Rio Mutum is a few kilometres farther on. For SESC, head southeast of Poconé along the unpaved MT370.

A more flexible option would be to hire a car from Campo Grande and drive north into the Pantanal from that city, Aquidauana or Miranda. There is good birding, for example, 33km along the road north of Aquidauana towards Barra Mansa and Tupaceretã, where a trail enters dry forest. Look here for undulated tinamou, golden-collared macaw, blaze-winged parakeet and passerine specialities such as Mato Grosso antbird. There are campsites along the Aquidauana River, 50km north of Aquidauana; at least one, Camping Baía, offers boats for riverine excursions. Wild camping is also theoretically possible. Alternatively, you can day-trip Fazenda San Francisco (page 140) from Miranda and get within 6km by bus. Outside Brazil, budget options include Puerto Suárez or Quijarro in Bolivia (page 149) and Bahía Negra in Paraguay (page 147). From Puerto Suárez or Quijarro, local operators offer day trips (and longer excursions) by boat into Otuquis National Park. From Bahía Negra, you can drive local roads at night looking for mammals and contract a local fisherman to take you onto the water.

Hyacinth macaws are hard to miss in the Pantanal, whatever your budget. (JL)

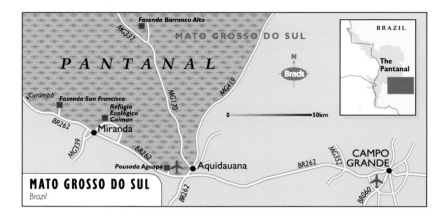

MATO GROSSO DO SUL, BRAZIL

The southern Brazilian Pantanal lies in Mato Grosso do Sul state. The best wildlife-watching experiences here are on a handful of well-run but widely separated and expensive *fazendas*. Access is from Campo Grande or from the nearer Aquidauana and Miranda. As there is no Transpantaneira equivalent that connects several lodges, it is less easy to organise a multi-venue trip. Most visitors spend several days at a single lodge. Unlike Mato Grosso, all lodges are open year-round (or almost so).

Wildlife is similar to Mato Grosso. The same core elements – storks, ibises, egrets, yacaré and capybara – abound. But there are differences; Mato Grosso do Sul is better for some species but not others. On the plus side, peccaries, pampas deer, giant anteater and king vulture are easier to see, and the chances of maned wolf higher. Isolated pockets of cerrado hold avian specialists such as white-rumped and white-banded tanagers. Macaws are more evident: as in the north, most lodges host breeding hyacinths, but blue-and-yellow, red-shouldered and red-and-green macaws are more likely. Mato Grosso do Sul is also better for blaze-winged parakeet and swallow-tailed hummingbird. Absentees include black-tailed marmoset, zigzag heron and chestnut-bellied guan. Although regular at some lodges, jaguar is generally more elusive, as are marsh deer and sunbittern.

Gallery forest in the Pantanal of Mato Grosso do Sul. (FP/FLPA)

WILDLIFE HOTSPOTS AND ACCOMMODATION

Fazenda Barranco Alto Ecolodge *(4 rooms; tel: +55 67 3241 4047 [messages] or +55 67 9643 6058 [satellite]; email: barrancoalto@gmail.com; www.fazendabarrancoalto.com.br; open Mar–Dec. US$230 pp sharing, inc FB, bilingual guide, all activities. Transfers extra)* lies 120km northwest of Aquidauana along the Negro River. It is owned, managed and inhabited by an agronomist–biologist couple, Marina Schweizer and Lucas Leuzinger, who pursue wildlife research and conservation alongside ecotourism. One-third of the 9,000ha is a private protected area; the remainder is a working cattle ranch. A research station houses up to ten scientists; wildlife research includes radio-collaring jaguars to learn about their movements. Marina and Lucas lead wildlife-watching activities, assisted by local guides. Two open-top safari vehicles head out by day and night. Visitors visit the Negro River by canoe or motorboat – the latter equipped with swivel seats so you never miss the action. Walk along numerous trails or traverse larger areas on horseback. An observation tower offers a different perspective. Of five hides, two are mobile and repositioned whenever something interesting is discovered.

One of Fazenda Barranco Alto's key selling points is its mosaic of *salinas* or salty lakes.

As is characteristic of this part of the Pantanal, *salinas* (salty lakes) and freshwater lagoons are interspersed with extensive areas of grassland, forest and wax-palm savanna. *Salinas* such as Lindoya retain water during the dry season and are full of insect larvae; this makes them a magnet for egrets, ducks, South American tapir and even giant anteater (the last almost daily during May–Oct).

Jaguars are seen 15 times in an average dry season, particularly by day along the Negro River. Both otters are seen daily here, while white-lipped and collared peccaries are common in forests. All four deer are present. Southern tamandua often forages in a mango tree by the lodge. At night, look for three opossums and crab-eating fox. Among interesting reptiles, Brazilian redtail boa, both anacondas and caiman lizard occur.

Just over 400 bird species have been recorded. Greater rhea and red-legged seriema patrol grasslands. Search the river for agami heron and bare-faced curassow. Scrutinise whistling-duck flocks on *salinas* for comb duck. Six macaws include hyacinth, red-shouldered and blue-and-yellow. Seven species of owl occur, as do eight nightjars and 16 woodpeckers. A good suite of Pantanal forest birds is present, including rusty-backed spinetail and pale-bellied tyrant-manakin. Tracts of cerrado are a highlight. Giant armadillo, the rare hoary fox and the leggy maned wolf occasionally occur, but you are more likely to see birds such as russet-mantled foliage-gleaner, collared crescentchest and curl-crested jay – all otherwise scarce in the Pantanal.

This intimate lodge is beautifully designed, with bare brick and dark wood giving a refreshingly modern feel. Bedrooms are spacious and stylishly furnished. Cosy communal areas include a well-stocked library and shady, hammock-filled terrace – the perfect place to savour *caipirinhas*, on the house. Free satellite internet is available. Meals include homegrown vegetables and homemade cheese, jams and breads.

Fazenda San Francisco (*9 rooms; tel: +55 67 3242 1088/3333; email: reservas@fazendasanfrancisco.tur.br or caroplcoelho@terra.com.br; www.fazendasanfrancisco.tur.br; open all year. US$190 pp sharing, inc FB, local guides, all activities*) lies on the west bank of the Miranda River, 36km northwest of Miranda. Occupying 15,000ha, this ranch runs a thriving ecotourism business alongside cattle ranching and rice cultivation. Unlike rivals, San Francisco is a regular destination for day trippers from nearby Miranda. The family-oriented restaurant caters for up to 100 hungry visitors, who may not see much wildlife

but certainly have a good time! There is accommodation for 40 people (at a squeeze) in colourful bungalows amidst well-maintained gardens. Bedrooms are simple, with fans rather than air conditioning. Amenities comprise a swimming pool, souvenir shop and museum.

The management puts considerable effort into wildlife-watching opportunities. On the São Domingos Creek, visitors use a *chalana* (two-storey barge) or canoe to search for giant otter by day or Neotropical

Keep an eye out for maned wolf in tracts of cerrado in Mato Grosso do Sul. (LC/FLPA)

otter (and twinkling yacaré eyes) by night. Vehicular safaris are in an open-top 4x4 with tiered seating. April–June is best for mammals. By day, you should see giant anteater, up to four species of deer and brown agouti. By night, the targets are ocelot (seen daily), crab-eating fox (visiting the lodge), crab-eating raccoon and Brazilian porcupine. Maned wolf is also regular. The jaguar strike rate is high: one in three nocturnal trips see one. Alternatively you could shun wheels and walk along several trails – including a gallery forest boardwalk – scan the horizon from an observation tower or scour the *fazenda* on horseback.

Birding can be good, with more than 330 species recorded. Four macaws include hyacinth and blue-and-yellow; blaze-winged parakeet is a speciality. In forests, look for great rufous woodcreeper, red-billed scythebill and Mato Grosso antbird. Scan skies for raptors, including black-and-white hawk-eagle. In common with nearby lodges, the owners are committed to wildlife research and conservation. Current projects include a study of ocelot ecology, jaguar and hyacinth macaw conservation initiatives, environmental education programmes and the rehabilitation of injured wild animals.

Run by the same family for 150 years, Fazenda São José remains a working cattle ranch, but today derives more income from ecotourism and sport fishing. Both activities are based at its lodge, **Pousada Aguapé** (*15 rooms; tel: +55 67 3258 1146/9986 0351/ 9986 1215; email: pousadaaguape@terra.com.br; www.aguape.com.br; open all year. US$120 pp sharing, inc FB, local guide and activities. Bilingual/wildlife guides extra*), 60km along mainly dirt roads from Aquidauana. The property's habitat mosaic includes cerrado, wetlands, lakes and gallery forest. In cerrado, look for rare birds such as cock-tailed tyrant and white-rumped tanager. Elsewhere, there are an amazing six species of macaw, six parakeets (including blaze-winged and peach-fronted), seven owls and five nightjars. Most usual avian suspects are present – from greater rhea to Mato Grosso antbird, and capped heron to rusty-backed spinetail. Among mammals, giant anteater is easy to see, often foraging for insects buzzing round lights in the lodge gardens. Pampas deer is relatively common, and most visitors see crab-eating raccoon. Other attractions include both otters, both peccaries, maned wolf (in the cerrado) and

A subtly charming parrot, peach-fronted parakeet occurs at a few Mato Grosso do Sul lodges. (JL)

South American tapir. Cats are scarce, but ocelot often takes top billing on night drives and puma is more regular than jaguar. Reptile highlights are yellow anaconda and red-footed tortoise, but both require luck.

Aguapé makes the most of its bounteous biodiversity. You can explore large areas of the fazenda atop a 12-seater safari vehicle or on horseback, and walk smaller areas along several trails. Motorboat trips along the Aquidauana River are particularly productive during the rainy season, offering a strong chance of South American tapir. Note, however, that activity groups comprise as many as ten people, more than most Pantanal lodges.

Bedrooms are stylish and colourful. An open-sided restaurant serves tasty regional food, and artwork liberally adorns intimate communal areas. Visitors may relax in a swimming pool, work off excess energy on the football field or even help *peões* with the cattle. For insomniacs, there is a games room, satellite television and internet. Like other major lodges, Fazenda São José funds charitable activities, such as a school for rural children.

Refúgio Ecológico Caiman (*25 rooms; tel: + 55 11 3706 1800 [reservations] or +55 67 3242 1450 [lodge]; email: caiman@caiman.com.br; www.caiman.com.br; open all year. US$800 dbl [mid-Jul–mid-Sep; bookings for 3–4 nights only starting Thu and Sun] or US$3,800/5,000 per lodge of 6/8 rooms [at other periods; no minimum stay]. Price inc FB most activities but exc optional excursions & transfers*) covers 53,000ha, of which more than one-tenth is a private nature reserve. The owners combine low-impact cattle-ranching, ecotourism and wildlife conservation. Caiman is a large, slick but well-intentioned operation, an understandable winner of recent sustainable tourism awards. Visitors stay in one of three lodges. Each offers something special: Sede hosts a glossy environmental education centre, the cosy Baiazinha lies on a lakeshore and Cordilheira adjoins the forest. All are attractive, with large communal spaces, swimming pool, bar, restaurant and luxurious bedrooms. Food is fresh, flavoursome and neatly presented.

University-educated naturalists help visitors explore savannas, gallery forests, wetlands and seasonal rivers. Converted vehicles transport you on safaris by day or night. Canoeing enables silent approach to yacaré and capybara. You can hire a motorboat to reach remote areas; the half-day trip returns after dark, spotlighting for mammals. There are a dozen trails, mostly in forest. You can also ride the grasslands on horseback.

Visitors to Refúgio Ecológico Caiman can relax in comfort.

Of 40 mammal species recorded, giant anteater and southern tamandua are regular in scrub near Sede, particularly in the dry season. In October– December, South American tapir feasts on fallen mangoes near the lodges. Other herbivores include all four deer, white-lipped and collared peccaries, Brazilian porcupine and lowland paca. Maned wolf, both otters and bush dog head the carnivore list. Ocelots often fish at Paizinho bridge – a great spot from which to photograph yacaré. Look for red-footed tortoise on land and Vanderhaege's toad-headed turtle in the water. Fifteen snakes include yellow anaconda and Brazilian redtail boa.

The range of habitats enables birders easily to rack up 180 species – half the site total – in three days. The entrance road is good for greater rhea, red-legged seriema and nacunda nighthawk. There is a chance of sunbittern, rare this far south. Five species of macaw include plentiful hyacinth. Blaze-winged parakeet is fairly common and 11 hummingbirds an excellent total. Helmeted and band-tailed manakins flash vivid red in the dingy forest undergrowth.

The wet season comes later in Mato Grosso do Sul than along the more northerly Transpantaneira. (JCS/FLPA)

Transport

Campo Grande provides the main access point; visitors arrive at the state capital by domestic flight or long-distance bus. The majority take advantage of road and/or air transfers offered by the lodges. Most visitors fly from Aquidauana to Fazenda Barranco Alto (R$1,000 for up to three passengers; the luggage allowance is a paltry 15kg). During the dry season (May–Dec, in a good year), you can travel by 4x4 (R$550 one-way for up to four passengers, six hours). Pousada Aguapé offers transfers from Campo Grande (R$660 return for up to four passengers, R$995 return for up to 15). Refúgio Ecológico Caiman runs transfers to/from Campo Grande on Thursday and Sunday (twice each day, taking 3.5 hours and costing R$162 per person or R$682 per vehicle). Fazenda San Francisco no longer offers transfers, but access is straightforward (see below).

You can reduce transfer costs by taking a bus (seven per day) from Campo Grande to Aquidauana (130km west of Campo Grande) or Miranda (200km west). From there, you can negotiate a cheaper transfer with the lodge or, in the dry season, hire a private taxi. From Aquidauana to Pousada Aguapé, a taxi costs R$240 return. From Miranda, one-way taxis cost R$170 to Refúgio Ecológico Caiman and R$60 to Fazenda San Francisco. Alternatively, for San Francisco, take any bus heading from Miranda to Corumbá, get off after 35km at the junction signposted to the lodge, from where you can arrange a pick-up – or walk the remaining 6km. A leisurely option is the new 'Pantanal Express' tourist train. This departs Campo Grande at 07.30 on Saturday, pauses for lunch in Aquidauana and arrives Miranda at 18.00. It returns the next day, leaving 09.00 and arriving Campo Grande at 19.00.

Self-drive is feasible but, unlike the Transpantaneira, offers little advantage, as lodges are so widely separated and similar in fauna as to make a multi-venue trip less worthwhile. Moreover, lodges do not allow visitors to drive themselves around the property. Lodges will provide access directions – although self-drive is not recommended for Fazenda Barranco Alto as the route varies with conditions and a GPS is usually necessary. Car-hire companies with an office at Campo Grande airport and/or downtown include Avis (*tel: +55 67 3325 0036; www.avis.com*), Hertz (*tel: +55 67 3368 6108; www.hertz.com*), Localiza (*tel: +55 67 3382 8786; www.localiza.com*) and Unidas (*tel: +55 67 0363 2145; www.unidas.com.br*). Expect to pay at least US$100 per day for a 4x4.

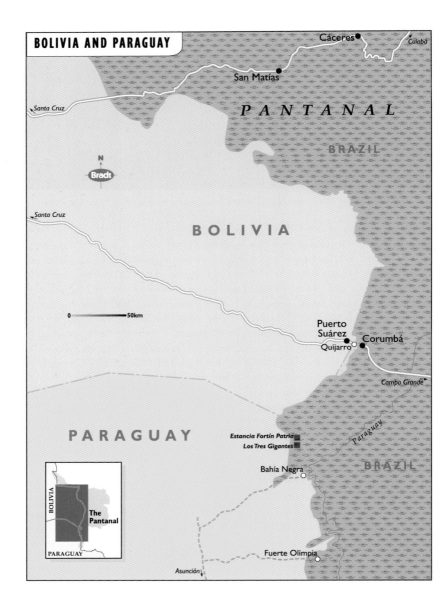

BOLIVIA AND PARAGUAY

PARAGUAY

One-tenth of the Pantanal lies in Paraguay, and much of this is ostensibly protected by the 123,000ha Rio Negro National Park. This pristine wilderness is heaving with wildlife, but most is inaccessible. Fortunately, two decent lodges enable the adventurous wildlife-watcher to experience the Pantanal's natural splendour far from the tourist crowd.

Wax palm stands flank the Negro River in the Paraguayan Pantanal. (EH)

WILDLIFE HOTSPOTS AND ACCOMMODATION

The core wildlife is broadly the same as in the Brazilian Pantanal. Some 340 bird species have been recorded. Herons, egrets, storks, ibises, screamers and skimmers ply the wetlands. Most Pantanal passerine specialities occur, examples being pale-legged hornero, cinereous-breasted and white-lored spinetail, rufous cacholote and Mato Grosso antbird. Marsh and South American brown brocket deer are common. Both otters inhabit the rivers. Forty reptiles include snakes such as yellow anaconda, slug-eating snake, tropical rattlesnake and Neuwied's lancehead. Yacaré are numerous; common iguana and black tegu frequent. The Paraguayan Pantanal offers opportunities for several species that are absent or less common farther north. Such mammals include white-coated titi and Chacoan peccary. Among birds, white-barred piculet replaces white-wedged piculet, while Bolivian slaty-antshrike takes over from planalto slaty-antshrike. Chacoan leaf-footed gecko, meanwhile, marks the Chacoan influence over the reptile fauna.

Lying at this ecosystem interface inevitably means that some Pantanal species, common in Brazil, are rare or absent in Paraguay. Among mammals, pampas deer is absent, capybara less numerous, and South American tapir, Azara's night monkey, the cats, maned wolf and white-lipped peccary rare. Among the notable avian absentees are agami and zigzag herons, bare-faced curassow, sunbittern, pied lapwing, hyacinth macaw, long-tailed ground-dove, cream-coloured woodpecker and helmeted manakin. Other specialities – green ibis, great potoo, peach-fronted parakeet, American pygmy kingfisher and rusty-fronted tody-flycatcher – are harder to see.

Probably the best base is **Los Tres Gigantes** (*3 rooms; tel: +595 21 223 567; email: guyra@guyra.org.py; www.guyra.org.py; open all year. US$130 pp sharing [2 days/1 night] or US$280 [4 days/3 nights] inc FB, boat transfers from Bahía Negra, nocturnal walks & horserides. Optional extras inc boat trips [US$55 per boat], land transfer from Asunción & bilingual wildlife guide [US$100 per guide, payable locally]. Complete package for 4 days/3 nights, US$790 pp sharing*), a 15,000ha biological station and reserve managed by the country's leading conservation NGO, Guyra Paraguay. The lodge name alludes to three gargantuan mammals present: giant

Los Tres Gigantes has a delightful riverside location.

otter, giant anteater and giant armadillo. It is easy to see the otter: there is a holt just 200m from the lodge. There is also a very good chance of the anteater, particularly from August–November. Although diggings provide evidence that giant armadillos occur, seeing this notoriously elusive mammal needs a big kiss from Lady Luck.

Even without the giants, there is plenty to see. Access to gallery forest, palm savanna and wetlands is by foot along two short trails (white-coated titi occurs 450m along the southbound trail), on horseback, or by motorboat and canoe along the Negro River. Arrange bilingual biologist guides before arrival. Nocturnal safaris are by canoe along the

Forked tongue flickering, black tegus are a common sight in Paraguay's Pantanal. (JL)

Negro River, and provide close encounters with yacaré. The river is good for common iguana, marsh deer, and, if water levels are low, jaguar. Black howler, South American brown brocket deer and greater rhea are resident. Snakes such as yellow anaconda, false water cobra and Patagonian racer occur. The best chance of the first is amidst riverbank water hyacinths from September–November. Black tegus and other lizards are prominent in summer. Azara's agouti, nine-banded armadillo and white-lored spinetail are common along forest trails. During a three-night stay, keen birders can expect to see up to 150 bird species.

Accommodation is in a rustic but pleasant two-storey wooden lodge, with capacity for 12 people spread across one large double and two rooms with bunkbeds; all have fans. Dark wood walls are decorated with local handicrafts, and hammocks line shady terraces. Electricity is solar powered. To visit, make arrangements through Guyra Paraguay; visits contribute to conservation.

The other major alternative is **Estancia Fortín Patria** *(8 rooms; tel: +595 21 446 890; email: fortinpatria@webmail.com.ar; www.fortinpatrialodge.com; open Feb–Nov. US$160 pp sharing inc FB & all excursions. Air transfers from Asunción & bilingual guide extra)*, a private reserve of 62,000ha. The lodge lies on the Negro River, overlooking wetlands, palm savanna and denser forest. A 600m boardwalk leads to the river and provides access to areas for Neotropical otter and reptiles. A shorter trail leads to a black howler territory. You can explore in canoes built by the local Chamacoco community and wander the property on horseback. In the dry season, 4x4 vehicles are used for safaris. The lodge can arrange bilingual wildlife guides. Wildlife is similar to that at Los Tres Gigantes, with jaguar, puma, giant anteater and giant otter seen relatively regularly. There is also an outside chance of bumping into South American tapir or maned wolf. The best time to visit is probably September–early December. Accommodation is in a large, attractive, two-storey wooden lodge. Bedrooms are simple and stylish; four are en suite. Substantial communal space includes an indoor swimming pool (providing respite from the daytime heat) and an open fire (offering warmth during the evening chill). Food is generally good, and vegetables are homegrown.

A cheaper option is the town of **Bahía Negra**. Staying in a local hotel, visitors can make day trips along waterways and nocturnal forays along roads. For the boat trips, you will need to negotiate with local boatmen. There is a good chance of giant otter, common iguana and Mato Grosso antbird along the river. In forest, look for white-coated titi, Azara's night monkey and black-tailed marmoset. At night, drive slowly along roads surrounding Bahía Negra, searching for mammals such as South American tapir, brown brocket, tayra, crab-eating raccoon and both white-lipped and collared peccaries. Mammal density can be high. South of Bahía Negra, you can also use the town of **Fuerte Olimpo** as a base. In the dry season, roadside pools hum with activity: typical Pantanal waterbirds such as jabiru, plumbeous ibis, various herons and egrets, and black skimmer gather to harvest dying fish, while yacaré and raptors, such as crane hawk and snail kite, also take advantage of easy pickings. Paul Smith of Fauna Paraguay (*email: faunaparaguay@yahoo.com.ar; www.faunaparaguay.com*) guides trips in this area.

Look out for crane hawk near roadside pools. (JL)

Transport

Land travel is time-consuming as poorly maintained dirt roads are often impassable after rain, even in a 4x4. The journey from Asunción to Bahía Negra takes 15–17 hours: fortunately, the section through the Chaco (particularly beyond Cruce Los Pioneros) is great for mammals such as puma, jaguar, giant anteater and even Chacoan peccary. For Los Tres Gigantes, take advantage of Guyra Paraguay transfers to Bahía Negra. Visitors hire the NGO's 4x4 (US$90 per day) and pay for petrol (US$375 return). The final access to the lodge is by boat from Bahía Negra, whatever the season (US$30 to hire; US$65 for petrol). Boats from Bahía Negra to Fortín Patria take 45 minutes.

If you prefer self-drive, international vehicle-hire companies operating from Asunción include Hertz (*tel: +595 21 645600/605708; www.hertz.com*), Localiza (*tel: +595 21 683892; www.localiza.com.br*), and National (*tel: +595 21 232990; www.nationalcar.com*); their vehicles are uninsured off paved highways. Local companies include Touring Automovil Club Paraguayo (*tel: +595 21 447945*), Only Rent-a-Car (*tel: +595 21 492731*) and Fast (*tel: +595 21 496054*). Expect to pay US$1,200–1,600 per week for a 4x4.

Public transport is inconvenient. There is a weekly bus from Asunción to Bahía Negra (Tuesdays, 18 hours, US$38). If time is no issue, take a bus from Asunción to Concepción (daily, five to six hours, US$15), from where a weekly boat leaves on Tuesday, arriving in Bahía Negra on Friday then returning the same day (*Barco Aquidabán; tel: +595 331 242 435*; from US$23).

You can also fly to Bahía Negra: a two-hour charter flight from Asunción with Airmen (*tel: +595 21 645 980/990; email: airreservas@gmail.com*) or AeroTax (*tel: +595 21 645 616/646 523; email: info@aerotax.com*). A five-seater plane costs US$1,625 for an overnight return trip; for US$200 extra the pilot will wait three days before bringing you back. A three-seater aircraft costs slightly less, and a twin-motor plane seats and costs roughly double. Fortín Patria can arrange a ten-seater Cessna direct to the lodge, for US$3,500.

Few people visit the Paraguayan Pantanal in summer (November–March), due to intense heat, oppressive mosquitoes and complicated access. During this period, road transport to Bahía Negra is impossible, so travel from Concepción by boat or from Asunción by air.

BOLIVIA

One-fifth of the Pantanal lies in Santa Cruz province, Bolivia, adjacent to the Brazilian and Paraguayan borders. This little-explored area offers the prospect of exciting wildlife experiences and even discoveries: who knows what will be round the next river bend? Unfortunately, the tourism infrastructure is rudimentary, with little choice of destination or service provider. Given the impetus that the Bolivian government and NGOs are now giving to ecotourism, however, this may change.

Much of the Bolivian Pantanal is protected in two state-run reserves: the 2.9 million hectare San Matías Natural Area of Integrated Management (*www.sanmatias-pantanal.org*) and the 1 million hectare Otuquis National Park and Natural Area of Integrated Management (*www.otuquis-pantanal.org*). San Matías has Amazonian overtones to its flora and fauna, while Otuquis displays Chacoan and Chiquitano elements. Indeed only one-eighth of San Matías and one-quarter of Otuquis relate to the Pantanal. Nevertheless, this leaves plenty for the intrepid traveller to explore.

From the few studies that have been carried out, the core wildlife is similar to that in Brazil and Paraguay. On a four-day trip, you stand a good chance of seeing both otters,

Red-and-green macaw is more abundant than hyacinth macaw in the Bolivian Pantanal. (PO/FLPA)

white-lipped peccary, marsh and pampas deer, black howler and yellow anaconda, as well as the standard fare of yacaré, capybara and waterbirds. In gallery forests, look for white-coated titi and Azara's night monkey. The farther from civilisation you venture, the greater your prospects of bumping into jaguar or giant anteater.

WILDLIFE HOTSPOTS AND ACCOMMODATION

In extreme southeast Bolivia, the unprepossessing border towns and free ports of **Puerto Suárez** and **Quijarro**, 15km apart, provide the starting point for boat trips into and around Otuquis. Day trips are the norm, but enable you to visit only the northern sector (the area designated for 'integrated management'). Entering the national park proper requires at least one night away (preferably four) and is dependent on water levels. There is no accommodation in Otuquis, so visitors either camp or stay in a basic fishing hotel in Porto da Manga, on the Brazilian bank of the Paraguay River. Nearly half of Otuquis is permanent water, so almost all access is by boat. During the dry season (July–November), you can reach the western fringes with a 4x4 by driving south from El Carmen, 80km west of Puerto Suárez along Ruta 4, or the southern sector of the park by driving to San Juan del Mutún, which lies south of Puerto Suárez towards Puerto Busch.

On a typical trip, you will visit several different habitats. In the grasslands look for greater rhea and giant anteater. The globally threatened crowned eagle inhabits palm savanna in the south; hyacinth macaw is very local, but blue-and-yellow and red-and-green fairly common. Stripe-backed antbird and cinereous tyrant – otherwise rare in the Pantanal – occur in dry forests. Azara's night monkey, black howler and bare-faced curassow inhabit riparian forest. Capybara and yacaré abound in the water, and one trip in two spots a lurking yellow anaconda. Crossing Lake Cáceres, look for jabiru, capybara, southern screamer, yacaré and giant otter. The Tres Bocas wetlands on the Pimiento River are good for marsh deer, occasional jaguar and abundant waterbirds. In the Sicurí, Tuyuyú and Tamengo channels giant water lilies astound visitors with their dimensions. This area can also be good for yellow anaconda, particularly in summer, as well as common iguana and giant otter. Other areas to explore include three other permanent lakes: Mandioré, La Gaiba and Uberabá.

Capybara are a common sight in the Bolivian Pantanal. (JL)

A few local agents organise trips around Otuquis. The best is the highly regarded NGO Hombre y Naturaleza Bolivia, which also runs **El Tumbador Lodge** (*6 rooms; tel: + 591 3 716 28699/339 6012; email: hynb_puertosuarez@yahoo.com or hynb@cotas.com.bo; www.hombreynaturaleza.com; open all year. US$16 pp sharing, B&B. Pantanal packages from US$366 pp sharing, for 3 nights*), 6km from Puerto Suárez towards Quijarro. On the shore of Lake Cáceres, these rustic cabins make a good base. The 380ha of dry forest hold southern tamandua and four primates. Puma, two otters and three species of opossum have also been seen. Birds recorded here but not in the reserve proper include hook-billed kite, ornate hawk-eagle and black-throated mango. Day trips are also possible to El Tumbador's forest.

Other places to stay include the large, plush and well-equipped **El Pantanal Hotel Resort** *(66 rooms; tel: +591 3 355 9583/3 978 2020; email: informaciones@ elpantanalhotel.com; www.elpantanalhotel.com; open all year. US$45 pp sharing, B&B; activities extra)*, sited atop a ridge at Arroyo Concepción, a few kilometres nearer Quijarro; it offers day trips to the Pantanal.

In central Puerto Suárez, **Hotel Casa Real** *(15 rooms; tel: 591 3 976 3335; email: walter_walterdorian@hotmail.com; www.hotelenpuertosuarez.com. US$15 pp sharing, B&B; activities extra. US$750 pp for 4-night Pantanal package, inc transfers, transport, biologist guide)* has clean, pleasant en-suite bedrooms. Its Pantanal trips include a package with three nights camping.

In Quijarro, **Tamengo Resort** *(6 rooms; tel: + 591 3 339 6542; email: info@tamengo.com; www.jodanga.com; open all year. US$10 dorm, B&B. US$17 pp sharing in private room, B&B. FB US$14 extra)* is the impressive Pantanal outpost of Jodanga Backpackers Resort's successful operation in Santa Cruz de la Sierra. Accommodation is in en-suite rooms that sleep six or in six to eight-bed dorms with shared facilities. Stylish communal areas include a bar, restaurant and swimming pool. Jodanga Tours, the in-house travel agency, offers Pantanal packages.

An alternative is to book through a travel agent, based in or near Santa Cruz de la Sierra. Options include Michael Blendinger Nature Tours *(tel: + 591 3 944 6227; email: info@discoveringbolivia.com; www.discoveringbolivia.com)* and Ruta Verde *(tel: 591 3 339 6470; email: info@rutaverdebolivia.com; www.rutaverdebolivia.com)*; the latter contract Hombre y Naturaleza. Finally, Bird Bolivia (the commercial arm of the BirdLife International Partner in Bolivia, Armonía) is developing a trip to see hyacinth macaws in the Pantanal as part of its excellent birdwatching tourism initiative *(tel: +591 3 358 2674; email: birdbolivia@birdbolivia.com; www.birdbolivia.com)*.

In theory, the cattle town of **San Matías**, on the Brazilian border 800km northeast of Santa Cruz de la Sierra, provides the gateway into the San Matías reserve in the north Bolivian Pantanal, which some consider could offer great wildlife-watching. In reality, however, ecotourist access is presently nigh-on impossible, with no local operators to offer trips. An emerging alternative is the town of Las Petas, c90km west of San Matías, along Ruta 10. The dirt road between here and San Fernando de los Pozones (80km south) offers good birding, with 10–20 pairs of hyacinth macaw plus white-lored spinetail in the gallery forest around San Fernando, as well as capped and boat-billed herons on the river just outside town.

Transport

Most visitors depart from Santa Cruz de la Sierra, 650–800km west of the Bolivian Pantanal. You can travel to Puerto Suárez or Quijarro by air or train. TAM *(tel: + 591 3 968 2205/2256)* and Aerosur *(tel: +591 3 339 9738; email: ventassrz@aerosur.com; www.aerosur.com)* each fly three times per week from Santa Cruz to Puerto Suárez (US$80–115, one-way). Alternatively, if you prefer your journey sweaty and time-consuming, you can take one of the Expreso Oriental, Ferrobus or Regional trains, one or two of which depart Santa Cruz each day *(www.ferroviariaoriental.com; 17–25hrs; US$7–35)*. Once in Puerto Suárez or Quijarro, independent travel options cease and the only way into the Pantanal is with a local or national tour operator.

TOP TIPS

Venture into wetlands on horseback. (LL)

FINDING WILDLIFE

In many ways, finding wildlife is a cinch in the Pantanal. Roadside ponds teem with yacaré caiman and waterbirds, while spotting mammals is easier than anywhere bar African savannas. Even a wildlife novice should have no problems in enjoying spectacular sights. But there is more to Pantanal wildlife than immediately catches the untrained eye. The region's mosaic of habitats rewards visitors willing to rise earlier, look harder and stay out later. This section offers some tips as to how to make the most of your Pantanal trip. It includes generic pointers on lodge facilities and managing your time, suggests strategies for particular habitats and provides insights into identifying mammals without seeing them.

Mobile observation towers can be positioned to offer visitors great views of wildlife, here nesting jabiru. (∝

LODGE FACILITIES

Lodges usually offer a variety of means to see wildlife. Walking along trails is an intimate way in which to appreciate nature. Horseriding enables you to enter otherwise inaccessible wetlands, but watching an animal can be hard when sat astride an impetuous steed. Vehicular safaris help you approach animals, either by open-top vehicle or saloon car. Boat trips are essential for good views of riparian wildlife. Observation towers and hides are an ideal place to while away an hour and see what wanders past. Most lodges offer guides for these activities. If you are keen to see a particular species, ask. Guides usually

Most Pantanal lodges offer guides, who may be trained biologists (*above*) or local pantaneiro residents (*left*). (Both JL)

know the best trees for primates, a tamandua's territory or a helmeted manakin's song perch. Some guides are trained biologists; others are *pantaneiros*. Both have their advantages. Biologists may speak different languages, carry equipment such as mp3 players to attract birds, and offer background about what you see. Locals tend to know the area thoroughly and are often extremely sharp-eyed.

YOUR PANTANAL DAY (AND NIGHT)

A typical Pantanal day capitalises on periods of greatest wildlife activity but allows you to recharge your batteries when things are quietest. Rising before dawn, you can look for nocturnal mammals before they return to their dens. A cacophony of black howlers and chaco chacalacas announces the lightening of the skies. Bird activity is greatest in the two hours following daybreak, but continues longer on the cooler river. As the air warms, reptiles emerge – but even they retreat to the shade during the heat of the day. As should you, taking a recuperative siesta.

As the sun abates, it's time to return to the fray. The last hour of daylight is good for large mammals, especially cats. At dusk, waterbirds and parrots flock to their roosts. As night falls, frogs vocalise, particularly after rain. If it is dry, nightjars will be active in the

Crab-eating fox spotlit on a night drive. (MU)

grasslands and forest edge. Night safaris are exciting: activity is greatest on warm, dark nights. Seeing animals at night is not as hard as you might think. A powerful torch is essential; the best are million-candlepower equivalents that plug into a car engine or cigarette lighter, and a green filter avoids dazzling mammals. Most animals reveal their presence by two coloured pinpricks: this 'eyeshine' is the result of a structure behind the retina reflecting your torchlight.

READING THE HABITAT

Each of the Pantanal's habitats poses particular challenges to the wildlife-watcher. A few simple strategies, helping you to look in the right places and at the right times, can enrich the experience and maximise the rewards.

Around the lodge

There's no reason to stop watching wildlife merely because you are lounging in a hammock. Lodge buildings and gardens hum with wildlife. By day, keep an eye on flowering plants for hummingbirds and orioles. Bird tables attract reams of yellow-billed cardinals, cowbirds and even capybara. Bats often roost in roofs, while lizards such as giant racerunners bask in sheltered suntraps. At night, crab-eating foxes may visit to feed on kitchen scraps. The post-prandial wander back to your room often reveals moths or beetles enticed by tungsten lights. In turn, these attract predators such as rococo toads, house geckos, bats and even giant anteaters. As you retire for the night, check your bathroom for snouted tree-frogs, which are fond of showers and sinks.

Wildlife around lodge buildings includes yellow-billed cardinals (left, MU) and snouted tree-frogs (right, JL).

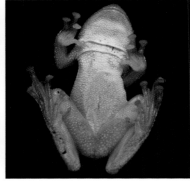

Anaconda crossing: always a possibility when driving through the Pantanal's wetlands. (EvU)

Wetlands

In lakes and swamps, it is impossible to miss seething masses of egrets, hordes of capybaras and lines of yacaré caiman. But careful scrutiny should reveal much more. Bridges provide good viewpoints, so approach them quietly to avoid flushing birds. Look underneath for roosting bats or a slumbering anaconda. Then scan the water, paying attention to well-vegetated edges for a skulking sungrebe or browsing marsh deer. If trees fringe the lake, check them for roosting black-crowned night-herons. If things look good, spend a tranquil hour or two, watching and waiting: who knows what might come to drink or bathe? In the meantime, look for dragonflies and damselflies flitting in waterside vegetation, check posts for swallows and kingfishers or examine temporary ponds for sleeping amphibians.

Catching fish to throw to giant otters, raptors and kingfishers. (JL)

Visit the same wetlands at night for a different set of animals. A crab-eating racoon snuffling round the water's edge, boat-billed herons fishing, a tapir grazing or – for the luckiest – a jaguar hunting capybara. Pinpoint individual frogs in the anuran chorus and illuminate them with a torch. Some species call from grass stems, others from inside the water. Drive slowly along roads passing through marshes; vipers, toads and crabs often use these as thoroughfares – and it is better to see them than to squash them.

River trips enable you to look for aquatic creatures and denizens of gallery forest. Most trips are by motorboat. Encourage your driver to take bends slowly to avoid spooking wildlife around the corner. The quieter your boat, the more wildlife you will see and the closer you can approach. Noise-free electric catamarans – in operation at one lodge – are ideal. Canoes are good, although photography is difficult if you're paddling.

Trips along narrow, well-vegetated rivers are the best way to see otters. Increase your chances near holts by gargling and whistling quietly; the noises often intrigue giant otters, which approach to investigate. You are sure to get close views of kingfishers and fishing raptors such as black-collared hawk, particularly if you have caught fish to throw them. Rivers provide natural vantage points for scanning the forest canopy; check flowering trees for black howlers and guans. On larger rivers, visit sandbanks for roosting or nesting terns, skimmers, pied lapwings and flocks of butterflies such as cloudless sulphur. Yacarés, iguanas and sometimes jaguars bask here (see box below). Finally, stay out late on rivers. Late afternoon is best for agami and zigzag herons, as they emerge to feed. Towards dusk, mammals such as tapirs and large birds such as bare-faced curassows come to drink. At dusk, river skies darken with band-tailed nighthawks and bulldog bats.

HOW TO FIND A JAGUAR

There is no better place to see a wild jaguar than the Pantanal. But even here the Americas' largest cat is hard to find. So how can you maximise your chances?

First, choose your location carefully. The Cuiabá River east of Porto Jofre at the south of Mato Grosso's Transpantaneira accounts for the large majority of visitors' jaguar encounters. The final 20km of the Transpantaneira are also very good for jaguars crossing the road. In Mato Grosso do Sul, Fazenda San Francisco has probably the highest strike rate of any lodge.

There is nowhere better than the Pantanal to enjoy close views of a jaguar. (MU)

Second, know your animal. The cat is active by day and night, with a peak around dusk and dawn. Take a boat trip or vehicle safari at these times. But also search during the day when jaguars are resting. In particular, maximise time on the river as jaguars love the riverside vista, breeze and hunting opportunities. After rain and on cold days, jaguars bask on sunny sandbanks to warm up. On hot days, they keep cool by lounging on an elevated, shady riverbank. Once a jaguar has found a suitable spot, it often spends hours there. If you meet people who have seen one, it may be worth heading to that spot, even several hours later. If there is no sign and you are feeling brave, carefully check the bank for tracks to see which way the jaguar headed.

Third, learn to look carefully. Spotting a jaguar during the day is not as easy as you might think. Dark spots and rosettes break up the golden fur such that animal and foliage blend with disconcerting ease. Also, train your ears to listen for the grunting alarm calls of capybara, which often indicate the proximity of a hungry jaguar.

Finally, respect the beast. If you're lucky enough to spot a jaguar, retreat a fair distance and allow the animal time to get used to a car or boat full of photographers.

Savannas and cerrados

One problem with wildlife-watching in open habitats such as grasslands, palm savanna and scrubby cerrado is that humans are highly visible – and animals perceive us as a potential threat. One solution is to use a vehicle as a mobile hide. When driving, stop and scan regularly, paying particular attention to shady areas where mammals may seek respite from the sun. On foot, use cover to conceal your movements. Another problem is the flatness of the terrain. Take opportunities to gain height, for example by climbing an observation tower. Scan for grazing marsh deer, peccaries, tapir and even the odd stalking cat. Check termite mounds for anteaters, armadillos and burrowing owls. And look upwards for soaring storks, raptors and vultures.

At ground level, look for reptiles warming up in the sun. Keep your ears open for the raucous calls of parrots as they fly between feeding areas. Drop to your knees to look for grasshoppers and green dung beetles, or to enjoy termite activity. Visit grasslands by night as well as by day: on a nocturnal safari, you have a good chance of South American tapir, anteaters, ocelot and, in some areas, maned wolf. And you should see nightjars sallying for insects.

Forests

Whereas tropical evergreen forests, as in Amazonia, often seem devoid of animals, the Pantanal's semi-deciduous and deciduous forests usually hum with activity. The dawn roar of black howlers is complemented by raucous chacalacas, repetitive forest-falcons and strident woodcreepers. Forest birds tend to be vocal, as dense vegetation means that it is easier to attract mates through sound than sight. Prepare for your visit by listening to recordings of bird vocalisations. Load cuts onto an mp3 player (or equivalent) and play back the voice of a skulking bird to attract it into the open. When it works, this trick can feel like magic. Whistled imitations of bird calls also often work (with undulated tinamous, for example) as does squeaking with your lips ('pishing'). Whistling the repetitive notes of a ferruginous pygmy-owl can attract a gang of irate passerines.

Use observation towers to get a panoramic view over savannas. (JL)

A whistled imitation of a ferruginous pygmy-owl may attract small birds. (JL)

Peering into hollowed tree trunks may reveal a roost of common vampire bats. (JL)

Listen for movement. Rustling in the leaf litter could mean an agouti or paca. Louder crackling may be a deer or peccary. Scratching in the bushes betrays a tegu lizard. Snuffling in the undergrowth signifies an armadillo. Crashing in the trees could indicate black-striped tufted capuchin. A loud tapping usually indicates a woodpecker; a softer version a tiny piculet. Soft contact calls may emanate from a group of coatis – and keep an ear open for the high-pitched whistle of the black-tailed marmoset. Sound is also the best way to locate invertebrates such as cicadas and crickets.

As you walk quietly through the forest, stepping over fallen branches and avoiding crunching leaves, look carefully at trees. Some lizards bask on sunny tree trunks. Common vampire bat colonies roost in cavities. The large, mud ovals attached to the trunks of large trees are termite nests. Trogons perch serenely on horizontal branches. A flash of colour is often a butterfly such as a morpho flitting through the mid-storey. Check for frogs in any microhabitat with water, from a flooded tree cavity to a rain-filled depression. Leaf frogs and tree-frogs live above ground, but poison frogs inhabit the leaf litter. Snakes often sleep beneath logs and planks, so turn these over with care (and gloves!). After rain, rooting in the soil may reveal a cecaeilian or amphisbaenian emerging from its subterranean lair.

Forests are great at night. Night-torching is best on foot, using a headtorch and powerful hand lamp. Use the headtorch to pick up eyeshine along the trail and watch the ground (you don't want to tread on a snake). Swing the lamp in a regular pattern; ahead of you along the trail (for terrestrial mammals, snakes, spiders and elephant beetles), into low shrubbery (for opossums, arboreal snakes and frogs), then up to the middle and upper strata (for night monkeys, owls and potoos).

MAMMAL TRACKS AND SIGNS

Whatever habitat you are in, looking down at your feet is also important. On sandy or muddy terrain, mammal hoof- and paw-prints are telltale signs of these animals' presence. If a set of prints is fresh, the individual that made them may still be around, so quietly following the trail sometimes produces dividends.

The size and shape of the impression enables you to distinguish between various groups of mammal, although beware that tracks of a species (even an individual) vary with gait, slope and substrate. The cloven hooves of deer and peccaries leave pairs of oval tracks;

Puma prints: an exciting, if frustrating, way to come across the Americas' second-largest cat. (JL)

in deer, these narrow towards the front. Tapir tracks are a trio of forward-pointing toes. Capybaras are similar, but toes are often joined by webbing – as they are on otters. The rear paws of anteaters resemble those of broad-footed humans, but the front paws leave an impression of their long claws; a southern tamandua also leaves a swishing mark where it drags its tail on the ground. Armadillos have three to five protruding toes. Coati prints have five toes, each with an obvious circular pad below long, slender claws. Canids such as crab-eating fox have four round toes, each with a short claw mark, leading forward from a broad central pad. Cats are similar, but their retracted claws leave no mark. The larger the cat, the bigger and broader the print.

Strengthen your claims to being the Sherlock Holmes of wildlife by looking for other signs of mammals. Droppings are distinctive. The scat of carnivores such as cats and crab-eating fox is long and slender. Deer and peccaries deposit neat piles of oval pellets. Tapir dung looks horse-like; that of giant anteaters is littered with termite casings. Diggings are another useful clue. A wrecked termite mound suggests the work of an armadillo; a mound with more precise incisions betrays an anteater. Mammal lairs are often obvious. A cleared area on a riverbank indicates you have found a giant otter holt. A strong odour suggests

Mammals betray their presence with faeces; this substantial pile 'belongs' to a South American tapir. (JL)

proximity to a fox or skunk den. A large hole may be an armadillo pad. A muddy wallow may be due to peccaries or tapir. And crushed grass maps out the body form of a deer.

PRACTICALITIES

A modicum of preparation will make your Pantanal trip easier and more enjoyable. This section offers advice on when to travel, what gear to pack and what health issues to bear in mind.

'Safaris' in converted vehicles are a good way to explore the Pantanal. (JL)

WHEN TO TRAVEL

The Pantanal is fantastic year-round, but cyclical water levels mean that wildlife-watching varies considerably with the season. Tourism peaks during the dry period in July–September. Wildlife throngs around scarce water resources, trees bloom, transport is usually feasible with a saloon car and temperatures are at their most pleasant. Jaguar sightings peak in August–September. Tables turn during the height of the rainy season (December–March): land becomes the precious resource, so mammals congregate on raised areas and visitors explore by boat or horse. Temperatures become very hot, and mosquitoes abound. As the summer draws to an end, during March–May, water scenery becomes increasingly beautiful. Most lodges do what they can to stay open all year. In the rainy season, this may involve transfers by air, boat or 4x4.

WHAT TO BRING

Wear lightweight clothing: cotton is good, as are new, breathable and fast-drying materials. Long-sleeved shirts and long trousers reduce the area of skin available to mosquitoes and other biting insects. Pale browns and greens are best, as they reduce your visibility to animals and enable you to spot biting insects quickly. Use insect repellent, be it DEET or citronella. Light hiking boots are adequate footwear, and sandals fine for boat trips and lodge buildings. Sunscreen, sunglasses and a wide-brimmed hat help ward off solar excesses. Bring swimwear if you envisage relaxing in lodge pools. A waterproof coat or poncho is an essential precaution (even if, hopefully, it remains unused), and both a windbreaker and jumper useful on cold winter nights.

For night safaris, bring as powerful a torch as you own; a headtorch is also useful when on foot. A pair of binoculars – of whatever quality – greatly enhances your appreciation of what you see and is essential for enjoying small birds. An mp3 player loaded with bird recordings is useful for voice playback or to check what you heard in the dawn chorus. A decent camera should be within most visitors' budgets; photography is a great way to capture your Pantanal experience. Don't forget paraphernalia such as batteries, film or memory cards, flash and tripod. And pack any medication you need; it's a long way to the nearest pharmacy.

Camera, binoculars and hat are indispensable – though only the serious birder will need a telescope. (KG)

HEALTH AND SAFETY

Health problems in the Pantanal change frequently over time, so consult medical professionals for the current situation. For example, malaria is exceptionally rare in the Brazilian Pantanal, with an average of one case in Mato Grosso do Sul per year, but there are occasional outbreaks (eg: 31 cases in 2003); it is more prevalent in Bolivia. Dengue fever may be increasing, particularly during the wet season; unlike malaria, there are no prophylactics. Yellow fever is also apparently increasing so vaccination is advisable; inoculations need ten days to take effect and immigration authorities may ask to see your vaccination certificate. Long clothing reduces the chance of mosquito-borne illness.

Chigger mites are an irritation, causing itchy red skin that can blister; they congregate where clothes fit snugly against the skin, but can be deterred by applying sulphur powder in the morning and having a soapy shower at night. One species of parasitic botfly (*ura* in Spanish, *berne* in Portuguese) targets humans, the larva burrowing through the skin and betraying its presence with a painful pink bump. Other diseases include Chaga's disease (transmitted by assassin bugs) and leishmaniasis (spread by sandflies). Bilharzia (schistosomiasis) is reportedly present in some waters. The Pantanal is a remote area with no medical facilities; the nearest hospital will be several hours away, at best.

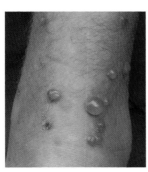

Look away now! Blisters caused by chigger mites. (JL)

Safety issues vary across the three Pantanal countries and in time, so read the up-to-date travel advice provided by your government (e.g. the UK Foreign and Commonwealth Office). In general, levels of crime and violence are high in Brazil, particularly in major cities – but most tourist visits are trouble-free. Few problems are reported in Paraguay or Bolivia. Low population densities mean that, as a rule, there is very little crime in the Pantanal.

Get down low for more intimate images. (JL/JMB)

WILDLIFE PHOTOGRAPHY

The Pantanal hosts wildlife in such abundance, and at such proximity, that few visitors fail to pack a camera or video recorder. But the type of machine you bring, and the ways in which you use it, are key considerations should you wish to produce a visual record of your trip that is as vivid and vibrant as the experience itself.

The digital revolution has given birth to decent 'point and shoot' cameras with an inbuilt zoom lens that offers magnification similar to a telephoto lens. Use only the 'optical zoom' element (avoiding the oft-hyped but low-quality 'digital zoom'), choose the 'action' setting (often depicted by a running man), and you should achieve some reasonable images.

For really decent results, however, it pays to invest in an SLR camera and a long lens (200 mm is adequate, but 400 ideal). The longer the lens, the closer you can get to an animal without disturbing it – and the larger your image and more relaxed your subject will be. There's something to be said for the compositional flexibility offered by a zoom lens (eg: 70–300mm), but they almost always lack the sharpness of a fixed (prime) lens. Swings and roundabouts…

Whilst longer lenses are a must for serious wildlife photography, they tend to be hefty. The heavier the lens, the harder it is to hold it still, so the greater the prospect of camera shake ruining an otherwise great shot. To get round this, consider several options. You might choose a lens with inbuilt image stabilisation; although pricy, they offer considerable advantages, particularly in low light. If shooting from a stationary car, use the window frame as a support, buffered by a beanbag or homemade equivalent (even a bag of porridge oats or bunched-up clothing will do). When walking or on a boat, mount your camera on a tripod or monopod.

Equipment, of course, only gets you so far. Technique does the rest. Wait patiently for the animal to get used to your presence. Shoot a moving animal on a fast shutter speed to freeze the action. For a close creature, increase the depth of field to get all of its body parts in focus. It may be easier on your knees, but resist the temptation to shoot a terrestrial animal while you are stood up; instead, get down low for a more intimate portrait.

Finally, ensure that you travel with all the paraphernalia that the digital world now requires. The Pantanal is not the place to be looking for shops that sell memory cards, batteries, battery chargers or portable hard drives.

FURTHER INFORMATION

There is plenty of literature about the Pantanal in Portuguese. English-speaking visitors, however, will find decent information harder to come by; travel guides to Brazil contain only short sections on the Pantanal and no book treats all three countries together. For guides to Bolivia and Paraguay see www.bradtguides.com. Field guides are best sourced through specialist outlets such as the Natural History Book Society (www.nhbs.com).

NATURAL HISTORY

MAMMALS

Guia de Rastros e outros Vestígios de Mamíferos do Pantanal. Paulo Lima Borges and Walfrido Tomás. Embrapa (2004). Illustrated guide to mammal tracks and signs, in Portuguese.

Mammals of the Neotropics, 3: The Central Neotropics. John Eisenberg and Kent Redford. University of Chicago Press (1999). Hefty academic tome synthesising the identification and ecology of central South American mammals.

Mammals of the Pantanal/Mamíferos do Pantanal. Fiona Reid. Privately published (2007). A double-sided concertina chart with illustrations of 30 common large mammals: a simple, portable identification source.

Neotropical Rainforest Mammals: A Field Guide (2nd edn). Louise Emmons and François Feer. University of Chicago Press (1997). Useful field guide to forest species, but omits some of the Pantanal's open-country species.

BIRDS

A Photographic Guide to Birds of Southern Brazil including the Pantanal and Atlantic Forest. Clive Byers. New Holland (2008). Photographs and brief identification text for 300 common birds, including many Pantanal species.

Birds of Southwestern Brazil. Balthasar Dubs. Privately published (1992). A catalogue and basic guide to Pantanal birdlife, with brief descriptions and stylised colour plates.

Pantanal: Guia de Aves. Paulo de Tarso Zuquim. SESC Pantanal (2004). Guide to the birds of SESC Pantanal reserve in Mato Grosso, Brazil; in Portuguese. Species accounts include photographs and assessment of status.

Aves del Bosque Chiquitano y Pantanal Boliviano. S. Reichle. Fundación Amigos de la Naturaleza (2003). Basic guide to birds of eastern Bolivia, including the Pantanal; in Spanish.

Avifauna Brasileira: Guia de Campo Avis Brasilis. The Avis Brasilis Guide to the Birds of Brazil. Tomas Sigrist. Ricardo Sigrist (2009) Hefty, two-volume bilingual work on Brazilian birds. More a reference book than a compact field guide.

REPTILES, FROGS AND FISH

Peixes do Pantanal (2nd edn). Heraldo Britski, Keve de Silimon and Balzac Lopes. Embrapa (2007). Technical identification manual to Pantanal fish, with colour paintings.

Serpentes do Pantanal. Otavio Marques, André Eterovic, Christine Strüssmann and André Sazima. Holos Editora (2005). Useful identification guide to Pantanal snakes, with photographs and plates; in Portuguese.

Field Guide to the Anurans of the Pantanal and Surrounding Cerrados. Masao Uetananbaro, Cynthia de Almeida Prado, Domingos de Jesus Rordigues and Zilca Campos. Editora UFMS (2008). Bilingual field guide to Pantanal frogs.

FLORA
Plantas do Pantanal. Anildo Pott and Vali Pott. Embrapa (2000). Hefty academic tome discussing 1,700 plant species recorded by the authors in the Pantanal.
Plantas Aquáticas do Pantanal Anildo Pott and Vali Pott. Embrapa (2001). Photographic field guide to 250 species of aquatic plant.

BACKGROUND READING
Pantanal: South America's Wetland Jewel. Theo Allofs. New Holland (2008). Sumptuous photographs accompanied by essays written by scientists from Conservation International. One for the coffee table, not the suitcase.
The Pantanal of Brazil, Bolivia and Paraguay. Frederick Swarts (ed.). Paragon House (2000). Essays derived from a conference on Pantanal ecology and conservation, summarising the region's problems and their potential solutions.

WEBSITES
www.faunaparaguay.com An excellent community website covering much of Paraguay's wildlife, including many Pantanal species. Includes a detailed online handbook to the country's mammals.
www.sbherpetologia.org.br Website of the Brazilian Herpetological Society, including lists of the country's amphibians and reptiles.

GLOSSARY OF PORTUGUESE TERMS

baia	Permanent lake (also known as *corixo*)
caapõe	Small area of raised land that remains dry while lower-lying areas are flooded
camalote	Floating islands of vegetation, often very large
campo alagado	Wet savanna or seasonally flooded grassland
campo limpo	Open grassland without shrubs or trees (literally, 'clean field')
campo sujo	Grassland with occasional shrubs and trees (literally, 'dirty field')
cerradão	As *cerrado* (see below) but with denser, taller woodland
cerrado	Wooded savanna, typically comprising slim, twisted trees, herbaceous vegetation and grasses, and often on well-drained, elevated areas
cordilheira	Larger equivalent of a *caapõe*
pântano	Swamp
pantaneiro	Human inhabitant of the Pantanal
peõe	Pantanal cattlehand or cowboy (*peón* in Bolivia and Paraguay)
planalto	Plateau
salina	Brackish lakes, typical of Nhecolândia, Mato Grosso do Sul, Brazil
vazante	Low-lying area; also used for the period when floodwaters retreat

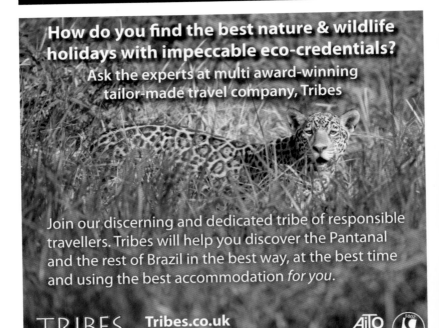

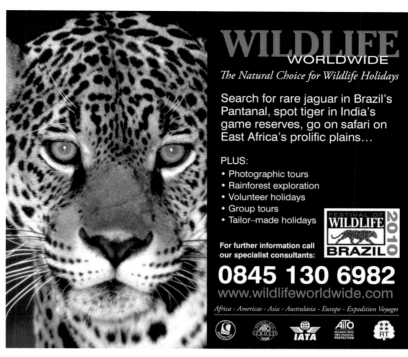

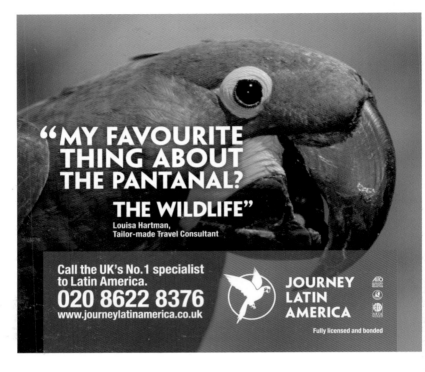